WHAT'S WRONG THE ORGANISATION ANYWAY?

MAKING RE-ENGINEERING HAPPEN

Eddie Obeng
MBA, PhD

Stuart Crainer

FT
PITMAN
PUBLISHING

PITMAN PUBLISHING
128 Long Acre, London WC2E 9AN

A Division of Pearson Professional Limited

First published in Great Britain 1994

First published in paperback 1996

British Library Cataloguing in Publication Data
A CIP catalogue record for this book can be obtained from the British Library.

ISBN 0 273 62220 X

10 9 8 7 6 5 4 3 2 1

Cover photograph: Tamsin Jarzebowska

Typeset by Northern Phototypesetting Co Ltd, Bolton
Printed and bound in Great Britain by Bell & Bain Ltd, Glasgow

The Publishers' policy is to use paper manufactured from sustainable forests

CONTENTS

1

UNDERSTANDING YOUR BUSINESS

RECIPE BREAKING

In a characteristically sage-like comment, Peter Drucker observed: 'There are no recipes for success, only failure'. Yet, recipes for success have dominated management thinking, writing and practice throughout the twentieth century. Good management is, and has been, available on prescription from business schools and management gurus. Generic business strategies propounded by well-paid luminaries have attracted many managers. They are told that if they do certain things they will become successful – or at least reduce the risk of failure. Complex issues, such as achieving competitiveness, are boiled down to four or five golden rules.

As we have examined in Part One, the prescription has failed to bring life to the corporate patient and has in no way prepared organisations for the troubles ahead. The more cynical might suggest that re-engineering is simply another recipe for success. It is not. It is a means of survival and, at best, of success. It demands that managers learn new skills, more flexible ways of working and that organisations shake off their traditional ways of operating.

Re-engineering differs from the plethora of fads and theories which have come and gone over the past decades in that it calls for fundamental rather than isolated changes. It runs counter to the traditional preoccupation with enhancing existing ways of working rather than developing new and radical alternatives. The conventional outlook has placed a great deal of emphasis on learning from neat packages of history. This tendency has spawned management education by case study which tends, with hindsight, to make management seem a logical and clear-cut art. In today's turbulent environment management is often everything but logical and clear – indeed, management has never been surgically precise.

Re-engineering argues that how things were done yesterday is almost irrelevant. Yes, we can and must learn from past experiences and mistakes (though this is something managers and organisations are notoriously inept at doing), but the lessons of the past are only practically useful if they can be applied to the new business environment. It is no good learning history if we now must study and master the international dynamics of tomorrow's technology. In the 1990s and beyond, more of the same is simply not good enough. Nor is improving and accelerating the processes and activities which have worked in the past. 'There's a very obvious set of conditions that plague most companies. They can see that doing what they know how to do faster and harder isn't enough to take them into the next century,' warns management guru, Richard Pascale.[1]

RULES FOR THE REVOLUTION

1. Success in the past does not guarantee success in the future.

2. How you did things in the past will not be how you will have to do things in the future – this applies to virtually everything you do . . . and think.

3. Re-engineering is concerned with organising work *today* in the best possible way to meet today's goals.

WHAT IS YOUR RECIPE FOR SUCCESS?

Most managers and organisations have some sort of equation in their mind as to what makes a successful business. They are usually simple – this means they can be used to motivate people and be easily communicated within and outside the organisation. BTR's corporate maxim, for example, is 'Growth the goal; profit the measure; security the result'. Some are more clinical. In P&O's annual report, chief executive Jeffrey Sterling has commented: 'We secure our future by achieving sustained levels of profit on the capital we invest. That is the only way.' Or, some might live by the credo that consistent quality leads to more satisfied customers and increased sales. Alternatively, those who have ignored the Total Quality Management (TQM) trend might prefer to pin their faith to an equation which runs:

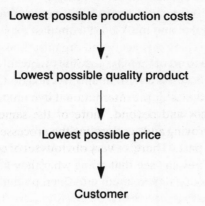

Lowest possible production costs

↓

Lowest possible quality product

↓

Lowest possible price

↓

Customer

In the boom years of the mid- and late-1980s, many companies followed this basic formula. In times of plenty, dissatisfied customers – or ones who are not fully satisfied and are, therefore, unlikely to continue as customers – can fairly easily be replaced by new customers. Perhaps the best known example of this approach is Gerald Ratner. Infamously, Ratner announced to the annual conference of the UK's Institute of Directors that his company's products were 'crap', as cheap and insubstantial as a pack of sandwiches. Colloquial, rather than customer-oriented, Ratner survived in business only a few more years. His family chain of jewellers has since been renamed.

Some organisations prefer recipes based on the assumption that provided they produce better products the customers will buy. One of the most poignant images of the recession of the early 1990s were car parks and even fields full of unsold luxury cars. At one stage Mercedes Benz had £850 million worth of unsold vehicles.[2]

Interpretations of why companies are in business and what they hope to achieve can be reassuring – chiefly because they simplify what you do – but invariably they narrow perspectives. They usually centre on a particular function or aspect of a company's business and are virtually never focused on the needs and aspirations of customers. Indeed, some appear to be built around a basic disrespect for customers. The end result is that the *potential* demand of customers is not met. Customers are used, abused and taken for granted, rather than developed and satisfied. But, what if companies took another view and started by asking what is it that customers really want?

Many already do this through rigorous market research, customer surveys and other procedures. The trouble is that though the data is there, organisations usually fail to transform their knowledge of customers into changes in the way they organise themselves or how they produce their products or services. The customer may be king but the corporation usually remains republican.

So far our discussion on recipes has focused on the role of the customer. In much of the literature reviewed in this section the customer is a key ingredient of any recipe. While the customer is traditionally granted primacy above all others, there are a number of other core constituencies with which organisations have to nurture relationships. As business competition increases, shareholders, the corporate owners are returning to the fore. The recent Cadbury Report on corporate governance is evidence of this trend in commercial organisations. Non-commercial and public sector organisations are also finding increased pressure on performance to meet their goals. Here, too, there is growing emphasis on satisfying the needs and aspirations of a variety of constituencies. Hospitals, for example, were once centred solely around patients. In the new reality, they have to deal with changes in customer expectations; fast-changing legislation; greater accountability to their 'owners'; relationships with suppliers; and a myriad of other issues. The core constituencies they have to manage have multiplied and will continue to do so.

Another emerging constituency is made up of legislative and regulatory bodies. Increasing globalisation and the formation of ever larger trading blocks across the globe, such as the European Economic Area and ASEA in the Pacific Rim, have given rise to a need for greater legislative control and regulation. Regulation levels which were familiar in industries such as pharmaceuticals are gradually spreading to encompass many sectors and organisations. Being able to meet this new pressure must become a significant part of the future recipe.

Suppliers are also gaining prominence in the new recipe. Organisations are slowly learning that only one organisation can be the lowest cost producer. This leaves all the others to compete on the basis of a slightly higher price and an extra differentiating ingredient. If this is the case, then for most organisations suppliers can no longer be chosen simply on the basis of price. Instead, suppliers must be selected on the basis of other attributes, such as speed of delivery or quality, which can then be transferred to the organisation's customers. Selecting and maintaining appropriate suppliers is now a key activity for managers and organisations.

Of these core constituencies perhaps the most underestimated are the organisation's employees. Despite exhortations from management writers and theorists, employees are often isolated from the process of change.

While customers, owners, legislators and suppliers are, to differing degrees, distant from the organisation, employees are at its heart. Their skills and their expectations are ever higher, yet they remain largely under-utilised. Even now, if a company consults its employees and receives a mass of suggestions on how it could improve performance, it merits an article in a management magazine. Involving employees is still news when it should be commonplace and automatic. The benefits are well chronicled. Legal and General, for example, solicited ideas from employees and, in 1992 alone, implemented 800 'projects for improvement' and a further 2,000 'opportunities for improvement' were identified.

The truth is best summed up in *Managing Talent* by Philip Sadler which observes: 'The long-term success of the business in attracting, retaining, developing, motivating and utilising the best talent in its field is likely to be the biggest single factor in determining its long-term commercial viability.'[3] As yet, few major western organisations manage truly and fully to utilise their human assets in the way Sadler anticipates. Increasingly, they will have to do so if they are to retain their competitiveness.

All five of these constituency groups, customers, owners, employees, regulators and suppliers, now significantly influence the chances of business success. It is true that traditionally, customers have been regarded as the key focus because they are seen to influence financial performance directly. However, the other four constituencies can also exert significant influence over corporate profitability or the ability of an organisation to meet its goals.

The growing importance of these various complex constituencies, each with their own expectations, makes it increasingly clear that the formulae and aphorisms which have served as reassurance to managers are now entirely inappropriate. So, too, are their recipes for their own personal success. The disappearance of career ladders, for example, means that careers have to be looked at under a new and harsher light. In this new climate, recipes for success based on the ingredients of the past are recipes for certain failure.

CULTIVATING THE CORE

How would you rate your organisation's performance in dealing with these core stakeholders?

Customers
- Who are your customers?
- How does your organisation listen to customers?
- How has it re-organised its operations to serve customers better?

Legislators and Regulators
- What kind of relationship does your organisation have with industry regulators?
- How does it communicate its concerns and ideas to them?

Owners (shareholders in the private sector; governmental bodies in the public sector)
- Who in your organisation has a relationship with its owners?
- How does your organisation communicate with its owners?
- Who knows who the owners are?
- What do the owners expect of the organisation?

Suppliers
- Who are your suppliers?
- Is the number of suppliers you use falling?
- How do you think suppliers regard your organisation?
- How do you communicate with suppliers?
- Is price the main talking point when you meet suppliers?

Employees
- Are employees at your organisation more highly trained than ever before?
- Do they have a stake in the business?
- How are changes and results communicated to them?
- How are their ideas for performance improvement gathered and implemented?

Others
- Who else should you be listening to?

WHAT IS YOUR ORGANISATIONAL RECIPE?

Amid this maelstrom of corporate and personal change it is easy to ignore basic questions and carry on as before. This is something organisations are highly adept at. Research has shown that companies can carry on blindly following a strategy based on a fundamental misconception for a number of years. Research at Ashridge Management College[4] found that 75 per cent of organisations were prompted to change reactively because of financial reasons; loss of market share or recession. Only 25 per cent managed change in a proactive way prompted by a consideration of future threats and opportunities and advances in technology. Organisations may see that the world has changed but appear immune to the logical conclusion that they too must change. Often they espouse the virtues of change and the need for change, but rarely does it inculcate an organisation. The way companies are organised is the most striking example of this phenomenon.

Organisations have traditionally been looked at as vertical structures. This has been the critical ingredient of the conventional recipe. Though organisations have tried many different ways of representing their structure, most, if not all, end up with some sort of vertical axis from top to bottom. It is a striking truth that today's organisations remain modelled on the principles described by Adam Smith in 1776.

Smith's fundamentals were later developed by the American FW Taylor into what became known as 'scientific management', a doctrine built around specialisation and the division of labour. Practical use of Taylor's ideas reached a high point with the advent of the mass production line with workers performing repetitious tasks on a mammoth scale. Management followed similar structures with different functions, such as marketing, sales, research and development, and production, being ruthlessly separated.

Mass production techniques reaped impressive early dividends. Henry Ford, the arch-exponent of the art, generated a huge fortune built on the increased productivity brought by mass production. 'It is not necessary for any one department to know what any other department is doing,' he propounded. 'It is the business of those who plan the entire work to see that all of the departments are working . . . towards the same end.'[5] Ford believed that managers should work in isolation, unencumbered by the problems of their colleagues, simply concentrating on what they are employed to do. Ironically, it was Adam Smith who identified the potential problem.

> A man who spends his life carrying out a small number of very simple operations with perhaps the same effects has no room to develop his intelligence or to stretch his imagination so as to look for ways of overcoming difficulties which never occur. He thereby loses quite naturally the habit of using these faculties and, in general, he becomes as stupid and ignorant as it is possible for a human being to become.[6]

The downside of such 'scientific' management is now well-known and accepted. Ruthlessly satirised by Charlie Chaplin in *Modern Times*, such 'science' brought with it worker alienation, a lack of co-ordination between different functions and a complete absence of flexibility. Any sense of individual responsibility was sucked away by the system. Imaginations were never stretched; intelligence was not developed.

Though the production line model of Henry Ford is disappearing and arguments over demarcation no longer fill the headlines, Taylorism persists. In the organisation of the 1990s, Taylorism has spawned a vast number of controllers, overseers and supervisors. Middle managers, planners and accountants have established themselves as middlemen between technology and implementation. Technology, brought in to reduce complexity, has more often than not brought with it teams of managers each intent on finding or creating their own place in the corporate order.

Hierarchies have expanded and new layers have been added with each technological step forward – note the growth of IT departments, strategy departments and so on. At one point, British Steel had an organisation chart which was so large and complex (and impractical) that it could stretch across a modestly sized office. Companies have preoccupied themselves with bridging the gap between management and workers or organising the workforce to perform more efficiently. Little attention has been paid to the role of customers; the layers of management or the core processes which enable the business to attract and retain customers.

Over the last twenty years great strides have been made in eradicating Taylorism from the factory floor. Management demarcations have, however, usually emerged unscathed. Re-engineering tackles white-collar business processes in a way that has never before been convincingly attempted. It seeks to bridge the gap between management and employees to create a seamless organisation geared around the needs of core constituencies rather than functions.

Sceptics of re-engineering may argue that the functional organisation works. Undoubtedly, it does. Companies have been organised along functional lines throughout the twentieth century. They have not failed, but they have worked inefficiently. The functional system isn't broken, but it needs fixing. The central problems of functional organisations are:

- **Goal setting.** Functional organisations set goals that are functional rather than business oriented. This means that groups of people in different functions have their own alternative targets and *raison d'être*. There may be overall corporate strategies and objectives, but they are effectively relegated in importance. A manager working in a functional organisation first and foremost requires that his or her function succeeds. Performance bonuses are usually related to divisional performance and managers are well aware that functions which succeed attract resources and the most talented people.

  The end-result of this is that the performance of different functions within the same organisation is often desperately uneven. This can be seen in companies which have developed excellence in one particular aspect of their business. They may well be financially brilliant, but overall their organisation is not achieving its full potential. A company with a fantastic R&D department may well be unable to transform ideas into practice thanks to a poorly performing production function.

- **Senior to junior process steps.** A business process frequently passes from one hierarchical level to another as it moves from one function to another. It is common that a junior person needs an input from a senior manager, a signature or some other task. In most of these cases the senior manager fails to take the work seriously. He or she may delay the work in preference to other work, even if the customer needs it urgently, or may make errors which the junior person has to correct.

- **Job definitions.** Harnessed by the restraints of their particular function, staff are overly specialised. The language used in one function may be unfamiliar or obscure to another. Usually the concepts they hold dear are at odds with the pragmatic demands of customers. Because of this they are unable to react to increasingly diverse customer needs. Instead of maximising the potential of people, functional organisation denies it. As a result, people become bored and frustrated, leading to higher staff turnover. Job definitions strongly reflect the functional nature of the organisation. There are few jobs – apart from chief executive – which bridge the gap between different functions (and the chief executive may well have a specialised fucntional background). Job titles are unlikely to include the word 'customer' in them. Those that do are vested with little in the way of power or seniority.

- **Responsibility.** In functional organisations customer service is not usually the responsibility of any one person. Any problems or customer queries spanning more than one department are passed on and on. Alternatively, problems are identified in purely functional terms – there is a problem with sales or an accounting problem. Identified in functional isolation they are solved in a similar style. At one organisation – pre-re-engineering – some salespeople looked after several hundred customers and an engineer typically handled around 100. Responsibility was effectively diluted until very little existed.

- **Communication.** The functional organisation is often characterised by Byzantine communication chains. Paper passes back and forth between departments. Delays are inevitable as in-trays become more full and customers more irate. The entire process is time-consuming and inflexible.

At Bell Atlantic a 15–30-day order-to-delivery cycle contained a mere

10–15 hours of actual work. The rest of the time was spent in waiting or was simply wasted as one department passed paperwork on to another. Similarly, at AT&T, a design cycle included 80 'hand-offs' from one department to another and 24 meetings. (After re-engineering this was reduced to 17 and one respectively.)

At Reuters UK, its prime customers in the City of London had to wait between three and six months to receive new hardware and services. Even if they didn't want hardware, customers had to wait two weeks. The process involved 12 departments and 24 hand-offs. Customers were further irritated by incorrect bills and some which were simply unrecognisable when compared with the original specifications.

- **Corporate Bermuda Triangles.** In the Pacific Ocean there may well be no such thing as the Bermuda Triangle. In corporate terra firma its existence is more easily established. Functional organisations often have stages of the process where no one has been assigned responsibility. Because processes tend to move to and fro between functions they remain unmanaged.

  One chief executive we talked to said that an important part of his job was identifying who has responsibility for what in his organisation. He found that managers were in the habit of passing things on to him when they were unsure of whose domain they belonged in. By abdicating responsibility the managers believed they had solved the problem. The chief executive then had to decide who should take responsibility for the particular issue. In effect, he found himself in charge of the Bermuda Triangle.

  The irony is that the functional organisation appears to offer clarity of responsibility. In practice it often overlooks the grey areas between different functions where no one takes responsibility.

- **Self-perpetuation.** As new functions and divisions are added to the basic functional structure, the old ones are never replaced. A company may have functional divisions as well as product divisions and, quite possibly, geographic, national, strategic and market-driven splits between different activities.

The process of self-perpetuation

Stage one: small and free of functional divides

Starting out, the company is small and managers fulfil a wide variety of different roles. The only division in place is that between management and production.

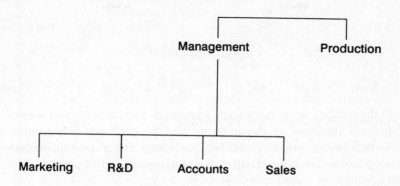

Stage two: functional divides put in place

As the company grows in size, it has to recruit more managers. It finds it easier to find managers to fulfil specific functional roles rather than searching extensively for multi-skilled generalists. It believes that specialists will enhance its reputation among clients, suppliers and investors.

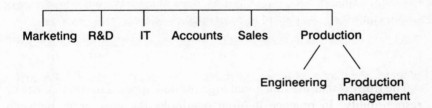

Stage three: product divisions added

The functional structure is causing problems. The people who have been with the organisation since it started find it hard to accept the new managers who adhere strictly to the functional divides. Everyone now has job descriptions and the functional heads are steadfast in their refusal to explore their boundaries. The business has not grown significantly despite the influx of specialist staff, the chief executive decides the trouble is that the structure is not simple enough. He announces that customer contact needs to be improved and so breaks the organisation into product groups – but the functions remain in place.

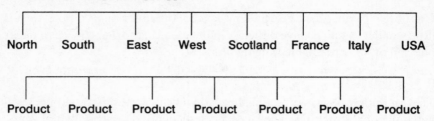

North   South   East   West   Scotland   France   Italy   USA

Product   Product   Product   Product   Product   Product   Product

Stage four: geographic divisions

The introduction of product divisions seems to be working. Customers are reassured as they are dealing with a smaller number of people. Internally, however, there is confusion. People are unsure how and when they can draw on the functional resources of marketing, R&D, and so on. Also, the marketing department has established a preference for two or three of the products to which it seems to dedicate a high proportion of its time and budget. The chief executive decides to simplify the company's structure. He brings in a team of management consultants. They tell him that he needs to target his resources geographically. He assigns geographic areas to separate parts of the business and appoints eight regional directors with specialist knowledge of their individual areas to supplement the specialist product knowledge of the product areas and the specialist functional knowledge of those in marketing and the other functional divisions.

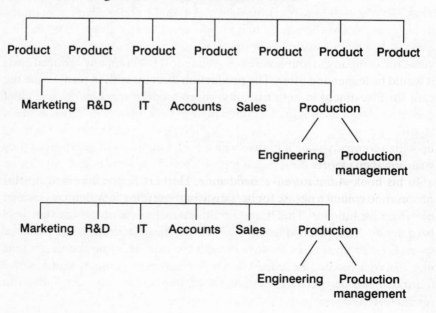

Product   Product   Product   Product   Product   Product   Product

Marketing   R&D   IT   Accounts   Sales   Production
                                                          /   \
                                                Engineering   Production
                                                               management

Marketing   R&D   IT   Accounts   Sales   Production
                                                          /   \
                                                Engineering   Production
                                                               management

Once organisations have reached this level of organisational complexity it is little wonder that they have difficulty in believing in the blank piece of paper beloved of some re-engineering theorists.

There is nothing new in revealing the inadequacies and limitations of vertical and functional structures. They have been recognised for a number of years, but attempts at breaking them down have tended to be isolated and short-term. Companies have turned to temporary project teams, task forces and various alternative matrices at times of crisis or to tackle specific localised problems. Once the problem was solved, they resorted to their old ways, continuing to gloss over the fundamental problem.

Functional organisations inevitably produce functional solutions to their problems. Functional organisations produce functional managers. 'The art of management is to promote people without making them managers,' Microsoft founder Bill Gates has observed – meaning that managers become hidebound by *managing* things rather than getting them done.

If a company is patently struggling, different functional heads will advocate different functional-based solutions to the problem. The marketing director will argue that the company needs to increase its invest-ment in marketing. If only they had more salespeople making direct contact with customers they would be better able to give customers what they want. They might also suggest that the sales team would feel more confident if they had a new glossy brochure to hand to prospective customers. The finance director is liable to shake his or her head at this point. From their point of view, the company's troubles are cost-related. If the company reduced costs it would be leaner and fitter. The production director will, in turn, argue the case for investment in better quality, more modern machinery. The chief executive, beset by arguing factions who are unlikely to ever agree, is likely to strike a balance – giving a little bit more money to each function or coming up with a company-wide initiative which each function will interpret as they wish and then ignore.

In his book *Administrative Behaviour*, Herbert Simon summed up this process and coined a phrase for it: 'satisficing' – settling for adequate instead of optimal solutions.[7] This is an in-built characteristic of the conventional functional organisation. Past strategy is fused with current organisational culture, so that people begin to believe that they know how things are done and stop questioning the assumptions behind their thoughts and actions. The recipe for success takes over and doubts about the company's ability to actually deliver success are automatically repressed.

> **Q**
>
> - Does your organisation have a rigid organisational structure? If so, how does it ensure that the product or service you provide gives the best returns?
>
> - How many people in your organisation are overseers, supervisors or controllers?
>
> - Given *carte blanche* how many people do you think could be made redundant without constituencies noticing?
>
> - Are business goals and targets set for individual functions?
>
> - Is competition between functions intense to the point of unhealthiness?
>
> - Does your organisation have a mission statement? If so, is it widely understood, acted on, and does it involve all your constituencies?
>
> - Do you have a job description? If so, how does it help you to deliver a better service to internal and external customers?

FROM EVOLUTION TO QUANTUM LEAPS[8]

'We cannot be satisfied to lay out a plan that will move us towards the existing world standard over some protracted period of time – say 1995 or the year 2000 – because if we accept such a plan, we will never be the world leader. We need rapid, quantum leap improvement,' Paul O'Neil, chairman of Alcoa, has observed.[9] In *Cycles of Organisational Change*,[10] Henry Mintzberg and Frances Westley identified five levels of comprehensiveness in organisational change. These ranged from incremental (minute progression) to isolated, focused, piecemeal (isolated changes in a number of areas) and, finally, *revolutionary* where change affects the entire organisation. Central to re-engineering is an appreciation that change must no longer be evolutionary or incremental, but now has to be revolutionary. Though revolutionary calls-to-corporate-arms are easy, the evolutionary approach and outlook is well established and difficult to change.

Interestingly, while the spirit of Charles Darwin lives on in our organisations, changes in the natural world are increasingly seen as having occurred very quickly through chance genetic mutations in response to dramatic environmental shifts. Evolutionary theory has given way to new revolutionary interpretations. The incremental, Darwinian approach manages change in a mechanistic fashion within an existing organisational or industrial framework or what has been called a 'recipe'. The end-result is what we label a 'directional strategy'. It is like a builder slowly building a wall, brick by brick.

The first assumption of the mechanistic approach is that time is linear and sequential – summed up in Heraclitus' contention that 'no man steps in the same river twice'. Many theories of organisational change portray the process as a series of logical, interrelated sequential steps. Along the way there are distinctive points at which the process begins and is completed. Change follows logical patterns within discrete time periods.

Change is also seen as inevitably delivering progress and development. Change is good. Organisational development, one of change management's influential models, has been described as the process of moving organisations from 'unhealthy' to 'healthy' states.[11] This has tended to mean the triumph of liberal and interpersonal values of trust and openness rather than any specific business or social outcomes. This view of progressive improvement lies at the heart of the mechanistic perspective.

A second major assumption of the mechanistic view is that change is an incremental process of adjustment. Periods of revolutionary change are seen as abnormal shocks to the normality of incremental progress. This assumption naturally leads to a belief that various social actors (managers and consultants) can deliberately intervene in organisational processes to produce a desired change. In a comparatively stable environment, engineered incremental change becomes possible. The plethora of 'cultural change programmes' and 'total quality initiatives' which emerged during the late 1980s put their faith in managing change in such a world. Despite mounting scepticism about the value of such programmes, managers remain committed to quick-fix changes which allow the transition from undesired to desired states. They also remain confident that they, along with consultants, will be able to deliver the required changes.

If change can be controlled, then managers believe it can be introduced in stages. Changes and initiatives tend, therefore, to be confined to a particular function, division or department. A company may perceive that its accounting department is too slow; it launches a quality programme to educate people on how to treat internal customers. Meanwhile, it is likely that other problem areas will be being dealt with in the same way. Gemini Consulting claims that it often finds as many as 300 initiatives in a single company, with up to 40 per cent of managers' time taken up by one or another of them. The end-result, concludes Gemini, is 'a lot of uncoordinated energy, but no discernible movement in any direction'.[12] A survey of 250 senior managers in the UK by consultants KPMG found that 35 per cent of the managers' organisations had run one to three major initiatives in the last three years; and over 25 per cent had been running ten or more initiatives.[13]

Q

- Why is your organisation in business?

- How would you sum up how your organisation thinks it can be, or is, successful?

- On how many occasions has your organisation re-organised or re-structured its operations?

- Did it succeed the last time it re-organised?

- How many performance improvement initiatives does your organisation have underway?

The third core assumption of the mechanistic recipe is the importance of maintaining a degree of *fit* between the organisation and the external environment in which it operates. The role of managers and change agents is seen as reacting to environmental change to ensure continuity of fit between the organisation and its environment. This notion of a 'gap' between the current position of the organisation and the pressures and imperatives of the external environment has been traced back by Henry Mintzberg to the design and planning schools of business strategy.

Within the evolutionary view of change there is also an assumption that the destiny of change is clear. Organisations have tops and bottoms; strategies have a beginning and end. In this view the organisation knows where it wants to go and then simply has to apply the appropriate sets of process skills to achieve the change. This is a *closed* view of change: both the desired outcome and the process skills required are relatively clear and determinable. Knowing both the 'what' and the 'how' of change assumes that the organisation knows enough about itself and its environment to predict and plan for the future.

In placid environments, organisations can build up experience through repetitive processes. They can prescribe both the 'what' and the 'how' of change. This closes options, creates order and makes the world appear certain. Where the future resembles the past, learning from prior experience may be appropriate. But, in rapidly changing times its value is less certain. As turbulence increases there is less opportunity for organisations to build on experience and then use it as the guide to future intervention. The past and the future are increasingly separated by a discontinuity. Both the 'what' and the 'how' are increasingly unknown and options are left open.

Generally, organisations have developed habits around closed change processes and periodic reviews of organisational position. In a turbulent world the use of closed interventions is clearly inappropriate, leading to unexpected outcomes, apparent lack of progress and a sense of disorientation, caused by frustrated attempts to define and re-define the 'what' and 'how' of change. As Fred Massarik says:

> We now face frequently, more so than even in the immediate past, that point of discontinuity where old rules – or even fairly well-learned approaches for dealing with conventional change – fail us. The force field once so neatly conceptualised by discrete and identifiable arrows, falls apart. Erratic turbulences embrace us. . . . The task of high-intensity diagnosis, therefore, becomes one of finding the way – for organisational development and for other purposes – through the paradox of 'regularity within chaos'.[14]

If change is no longer a process of logical steps, and needs to be revolutionary rather than incremental, then it consists of moving in a *direction* rather than toward a defined endpoint. Instead of having a closed view of change, managers now require an open view, acknowledging that the precise outcome of the intended change may not be known in advance even though the general direction of change is. Similarly, the organisation may not have developed, or does not possess, the necessary skills to handle such open change.

This view can be applied to organisational learning. In the simple mechanistic view, considerable value was attached to accumulated learning arising from the organisation's experience. To accelerate the learning process, in the re-formulated models, much more stress is placed on stimulating the organisation's capacity to learn from new experiences, its own and others, and on its need to experiment and then to reflect. Managers in the organisation are much less clear about either the final destination of the change or the means of getting there, but they believe if they learn quickly enough they will find ways to overcome obstacles on the road to change. There is also a recognition that the destination may be less important than the learning, or, indeed, the process of learning to learn, that takes place on the journey. This radical and dynamic approach to change can be seen as one of 'creating change' in response to Mintzberg's idea of 'emerging strategy'. It is like a child spinning a top. The child attempts to intervene in a dynamic situation to steer the object in a particular direction. The role of the change agent is similar – they are high-speed interventionists.

A central assumption of a radical or dynamic change perspective is that environments are neither placid nor turbulent. Instead, they are better seen as chaotic. Organisational literature has been paying increasing attention to chaos, often from a highly scientific perspective. Chaos is argued to be a fundamental property of all non-linear feedback systems, including organisations. A key feature of chaos is instability and unpredictability. The future is unknowable.

Perhaps more reassuring is the growing popularity for the idea of self-organisation. This theory argues that when a system is deeply unstable it can make a quantum leap forward to a state of higher organisational complexity. An example of this is heating a pan of water. When the water is heated carefully, at a crucial point it changes from a featureless regular substance to a pattern of hexagons. If the water is heated further it will boil. From a corporate point of view this process could follow the stages shown in Table 11.1. The period between relative stability and complete boiling chaos is one of mysterious self-organisation. This has been labelled the edge of chaos, a state where, if we apply the idea to business, companies are on the verge of instability but retain their ability to be creative and adapt to changing circumstances.

Re-engineering is concerned with fulfilling the potential of the edge of chaos. The revolutionary process of change involved in re-engineering turns established correct rules into old wrong rules. It can occur by the organisation, as a whole, altering a key parameter which defines and constrains it, or by the organisation selecting a completely new way to define its objectives and its ways of achieving them. Either approach will cause the type of paradigm shift expected of revolutionary change.

Changing attitudes to change

The core assumptions made by the majority of managers and organisations about change processes need to be challenged and re-written:

- We should not assume that there is an end-point to any organisational change process.
- We should realise that it may be impossible to know any more than the initial direction of change.

Table 11.1

Stage	Event	State of the organisation	Characteristics
1	Evolving markets. Stable customer base.	Stable	Managers confident of predicting the future. Workforce growing in numbers and highly motivated. Healthy balance sheets.
2	Technological innovation. Growing customer expectations. New competition.	Stable	Managers sceptical of changes elsewhere. Workforce and management dismissive of new technology. Small number of customers lost.
3	Competition increases.	Reacting	Quality initiatives launched in one factory. New marketing director appointed. Larger numbers of customers lost.
4	New legislation. New wave of innovation.	Edge of chaos	Redundancies announced. New management team brought in. Quality initiatives spread. Re-structuring begins. Adapting and creating solutions. Flexible working arrangements.
5	Changes in major market. More competition. Technology.	Chaos	Panic.

• We should realise that attempts to define precisely either the direction or destination of change using sophisticated planning techniques are, at best, irrelevant and, at worst, counter-productive.

- We should not assume that there is an existing and definable tool-kit of change methods which will work, even if we use them contingently.
- We should not assume that there will be any simple, or even necessary, link between our actions in change interventions and any organisational effects.
- We should not assume that it is possible, or desirable, to identify a recipe or map for the organisational and environmental contexts we may find ourselves in.

WHAT DOES THE RE-ENGINEERED ORGANISATION LOOK LIKE?

Re-engineering treats nothing as sacred and any process, resource or idea that stands in the way of satisfying the customer is eliminated: old job titles are dispensed with; organisational arrangements and structures are not merely tinkered with, but radically re-aligned; the methods of mass production, revered and habitual procedures, are rigorously scrutinised and abandoned. 'Business re-engineering isn't about fixing anything. Business re-engineering means starting all over, starting from scratch', argue James Champy and Michael Hammer in their book, *Re-engineering the Corporation*.[15] At this point the manager in the real world of pragmatism and compromise is likely to shake his or her head. How can modern, highly complex organisations take a blank piece of paper and start again as if the past never happened?

The managers are right to be sceptical. The blank sheet of paper does not exist. It is a dramatic image to convey the nature of re-engineering. But, despite the dramatic flourish, the process of self-analysis and questioning involved in re-engineering does effectively create a new type of organisation. 'Reinvention is not changing what is, but creating what isn't,' observes Richard Pascale.[16] Instead of accepting certain tasks as inevitable, re-engineering requires managers to ask why they are doing a particular task so they can dispense with work that does not contribute to goals, or simply does not need to be done.

Re-engineering seeks to solve the problems created by functional orientation. It replaces the vertical axis of hierarchy. Instead, re-engineering looks on organisations as a collection of horizontal processes. Traditional hierarchies fall away under the burden of self-examination. Rather than needing an entire office to house a complex organisational chart, layers are sparse. The American retail chain Wal-Mart, for example, has a mere three layers in its hierarchy to support a turnover in excess of $30 billion.

Although organisational structures are flattened and extended to ratios of 1:20 and more, the goal of re-engineering is not to flatten structures. Talk of flat or horizontal structures still assumes the existence of a hierarchy. Instead, re-engineering produces a fist-full of dynamic processes more akin to writhing snakes.

Of course, the elimination of hierarchies has been a notable trend of the early 1990s. Huge swathes have been cut through traditional middle management. Take one day's news from the world's companies. On Friday 14 January 1994, the *Financial Times* reported that GTE in the US planned 17,000 job losses over the next three years (due to its re-engineering programme); Procter & Gamble announced the closure of four plants and the loss of 1,800 jobs (re-structuring); British Aerospace cut 580 jobs (to 'reduce costs and improve competitiveness'); and the banking group TSB announced plans to reduce its workforce by 1,000 during the year, mainly in its administrative functions. There is similar news on most other days of the year, with organisations throughout the world re-structuring or introducing labour-saving technology. Often the redundancies appear to be cases of organisations taking an indiscriminate swipe at a monster of their own creation. If an organisation can make ten per cent of its managers redundant what have they been doing for all their years of employment? And, how well does the organisation truly understand the skills they dispense with? Mass redundancies do not constitute re-engineering. There are many companies where layers of hierarchy have been removed to leave a re-constituted vertical hierarchy. There are less people, but the organisational ground rules remain the same. In time, it is likely that the layers of management will return.

It is also worth noting that re-engineering does not necessarily involve job losses. IBM Credit, for example, now handles 100 times as many deals as it did before it re-engineered itself and employs only slightly less people. In the US, insurance group Capital Holdings reduced its claims-processing staff from 1,900 to 1,100 while increasing business by 25 per cent, and Hills Pet Foods (part of Colgate Palmolive) re-engineered its production process and increased productivity by 50 per cent over four years. In both these cases the companies were able to re-assign displaced workers through growth in other areas of the business.

We believe re-engineering seeks to create a virtuous circle (See Figure 11.1).

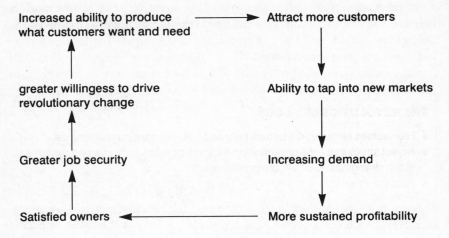

Figure 11.1

To achieve this virtuous circle, instead of the conventional pyramid organisation, the re-engineered company takes on radical new shapes. The brokerage arm of Merrill Lynch in the US has eliminated regional offices through IT to link 480 sales offices to headquarters. Andersen Consulting has created a web structure to interlink 40,000 professionals and provide access to specialist knowledge across 200 countries. Increasingly, organisations use the terminology of networks and webs to describe how they have brought people, inside and outside, closer together.

They are continually in search of new images to describe how they would like to organise themselves. Gareth Morgan, author of *Imaginization,*[17] champions the use of multifarious images to conjure up the organisations of the future. In one instance he uses the image of a spider plant to portray an organisation – it has a parent plant and numerous off-shoots joined by umbilical cords, and creates organic growth in a local environment. In their book, *Collaborating to Compete*, McKinsey consultants Joel Bleeke and David Ernst take an alternative view. 'Global corporations of the future will be rather like amoebas,' they contend. 'The amoeba is always changing shape, taking and giving with the surroundings, yet it always retains its integrity and identity as a unique creature.'[18]

Not every organisation may wish to be compared to a spider plant, a fist-full of writhing snakes or an amoeba. They are, however, examples of the kind of radical imagery and thinking necessary for organisations to re-invent themselves. If organisational structures are to be re-invented the language of organisations also needs to change to reflect organisational flexibility geared round key constituencies rather than structures created by managers for their own convenience.

THE REVOLUTIONARY LOOK

- Hierarchies eliminated – unless they add value to core constituencies.
- No set structures – the organisation must change its structures and systems to fit the changing needs of core constituencies.
- Process-oriented – the emphasis is on the processes which produce satisfied customers rather than functions.
- Horizontal not vertical – top managers are no longer distanced by way of seniority from the reality of satisfying customers.

WHAT DOES THE RE-ENGINEERED ORGANISATION DO?

The family-run Stone Container Corporation of Chicago would appear to have little need to re-invent itself for the future. Its profitability grew 15-fold in the 1980s, boosting annual sales to $5.5 billion. Yet, speaking at the 1993 meeting of the International Strategic Management Society, the company's president and chief executive, Roger Stone, described how his company is revitalising itself. The keys to modern corporate learning and trans-formation, according to Stone, are: to become even more 'customer-driven' and quality-focused; to stimulate innovation throughout the company; to measure corporate and individual performance on every possible dimension; to 'manage backwards from the future, rather than short-term'; to simplify structures and processes; and, most importantly, to foster a process of 'creative discontent' within the company. Stone concluded: 'If you want to be content you should be a dog.'[19]

Similarly unwilling to accept the dog's life was Reuters in the UK. In 1990 Reuters' new managing director, John Parcell, was deluged with customer complaints. Part of the trouble was several departments independently dealt with subscribers to the company's information services. Mistakes were rife and market share was falling. Reuters' re-engineering process began by breaking the organisation into four geographic divisions. These, it was hoped, would enable the company to become closer to customers. Each division was then sub-divided into a series of small multifunctional 'account teams' made up of account managers, planning engineers and business administrators. These teams involved three to six people who worked together. They were then given their own customers – between six and 50, depending on the size of the customer's business. What differentiates the Reuters teams from the ones usually introduced by companies is that they have no designated leader and they are permanent.

Reuters then tackled the customer order life-cycle, the process of moving from an order to installation and payment. This was re-designed with some steps – such as order taking and the issue of contracts – being condensed. The number of hand-offs in this process was reduced from 24 to four. In addition, Reuters has totally re-appraised its records and introduced an up-to-date computer system. The end-result is that more than 95 per cent of installations are on time. Customers now have to wait three to four weeks – rather than months – for hardware and services and barely a day if they solely order services. The company's billing process, previously consistently inaccurate, has now reached 98 per cent accuracy.[20]

What is notable in these and other examples is that companies need to be proactive. Rather than waiting for the crunch to come they have to set their own agenda for the future. As history has consistently proved, organisations which rest on their laurels – be they vast empires or makers of automotive parts – usually fall by the wayside.

The Milk Marketing Board of England and Wales (MMB) is a statutory monopoly supplier, the sole source of domestic milk supply for dairy companies. By 1990 the MMB had a turnover in excess of 2 billion, over 1,000 employees, over 35,000 suppliers and around 340 customers. 'We had a reputation with our farmers for security and reliability,' says MMB's Angela Shutt. 'But, we had established systems and processes which had grown around entrenched departmental structures over nearly 60 years and our reputation in the market place was based on control and bureaucracy.' The MMB has since been involved in a process of radical proactive change.

Pressure was growing for change among government, regulators and customers. The key driving force, however, came with the appointment of a new chief executive, Andrew Dare, who regarded the situation as an opportunity rather than a potential disaster and accelerated the programme of change. MMB took proactive action and suggested it be abolished, leaving the way open for a free market. In its place would be a dairy farmer co-operative which would compete against other companies. To support this idea, MMB set about changing its own internal operations which would be inherited by the new co-operative. Angela Shutt began planning the framework and scope of the project. There were three core issues she had to address:

- The pressure for change was such that MMB could no longer do nothing.
- MMB's functional organisation with fragmented departmental structures and bureaucracies could not survive in a free competitive market.
- Flexibility and effectiveness had to be increased at the same time as reducing overheads and costs.

'We decided that a process approach which reflected the cross-functional business process would deliver significant operational and cultural benefit for the organisation,' she recalls. 'We had to deliver an organisation where excellence replaced statute.'

MMB set out to marry its organisational objectives with the central operational and business processes. A group of senior business managers – called 'Champions' – were drawn from the company's key business areas and, within six weeks, established a strategy and process framework. The speed of the programme was identified as an important ingredient in converting people from apprehensive 'targets' into enthusiastic 'sponsors'. Momentum was further built up through workshops where managers could put their individual views on the process framework.

Central to re-engineering at MMB was an appreciation that it had to satisfy two key constituencies – customers (the milk buyers) and members (dairy farmers) along with government, consumers and other lobbying groups. Another important appreciation was that management parochialism, fuelled by functional divides, had to be eradicated. This was labelled 'pitshaft management'. The processes were seen as a means of linking managers across the black depths of their self-created pitshafts.

The group of champions continued to play a leading role as the programme unfolded. Managers from the group were made process owners and made accountable to re-design processes across functions. Work groups were also set up, drawing on people from throughout the organisation. All the teams were provided with training and continuous support. 'We explored each of our processes in terms of the current state and a vision, and saw we were embarking on a journey to transform our organisation,' says Angela Shutt. 'There was awareness of the need to change so we had to focus on the vision first. Once this was articulated, it fuelled enthusiasm and the need to understand the current state in order to start the journey became clear.'

The MMB's overall vision was broken down into visions for each individual process. The current state of each process was then analysed. This involved three main areas:

- people – skills, culture and organisational structure;
- process – customer focus, competitive advantage, process capability and flexibility;
- technology – applications and infrastructure.

This clarified the gaps between the current state of the organisation and its vision. While some processes required modest changes, others demanded complete re-engineering if they were to break through functional divides and meet the organisational goals.

Each team then had to come up with a solution to the problems they had identified in each individual process. The conclusions are now being implemented. The end-result, believes Angela Shutt, is clearer customer focus and improved customer services. For MMB members the programme has brought clearer focus, improved services and increased financial return. Within the organisation she points to a lower and variable cost base, improved process performance, new process capabilities and flexibility for future change.

The critical success factors in the MMB programme appear to have been: visible and clear top management commitment; early establishment of goals and values and clear communication of the need to change; the effectiveness of the champions' groups; and a core team of expertise to provide focus and support through sound project management. Along the way, the MMB re-engineering programme encountered many problems commonly experienced by other organisations going through similar processes. 'The largest barrier to getting started was freeing up the time of individuals to work on the initiatives. The very people we needed were also required to maintain current business operations,' says Angela Shutt. 'For the same reason, as the programme progressed, it became difficult to sustain visible senior management commitment. During the early stage, secrecy surrounding our plans made communication with staff difficult and constrained our ability to seek feedback from customers – who will become our competitors.'

The sting in the tale for the MMB is that having worked to a tight deadline when they believed competition might be introduced, the UK government eventually delayed plans to open the market to competition and the transformation of MMB into Milk Marque. Even so, it has emerged as a more flexible organisation with a clear idea of its goals and the tasks required to reach them.

The initiatives at Reuters and the MMB, as well as the aspirations of the Stone Container Corporation, give some idea of the scope of change involved in re-engineering. Gemini Consulting has developed what it calls the 'Four Rs of business transformation' which give another perspective on the full range of re-engineering. Gemini's 'Four Rs' are: re-framing corporate issues; re-structuring the company; revitalising the organisation; and reviewing the business and people. The key, according to Gemini, is to move along all four dimensions simultaneously, although not necessarily at the same speed.[21] The end-result, the re-engineered company, often has the following characteristics:

- converting tension to energy;
- contact with customers;
- responsibility;
- teams;
- flexible work.

1. Converting tension to energy

The traditional organisation is beset by tensions between different departments, systems, styles and people. Those tensions are often regarded as productive, a means of keeping people alert, but, in reality, their effect is usually negative. Frequently these tensions can be divided into the following.

Processes

Certain processes are formal and standardised. Typically these include generating invoices or ordering from suppliers. Other processes, however, remain highly flexible: they are unwritten and informal. One particular supplier, for example, might have an excellent relationship with the organisation's purchasing manager to the extent that many of the normal standardised procedures are circumvented and they work together. Such exceptions merely produce extra tension in the organisation and are interpreted as too cosy or preferential. When people breach standard processes there is an outpouring of despair from the guardians of the processes – the fact that a flexible response was necessary to keep a customer satisfied is often ignored. The emphasis is on being process guardians, indomitable protectors, rather than energetic champions.

Management

Increasingly, managers in traditional organisations find themselves in an uncomfortable grey area between autocratic and participative forms of management. While managers talk about empowerment, for example, they are at the same time often making decisions in response to the tough realities of economics in a manner that suggests a more autocratic, if not exploitative, style. Managers may not consider themselves to be dictatorial, but neither are they willing to surrender much of what they regard as their power-base to become participative.

Such tension is at the heart of many of the managerial failures of the 1980s. Managers were enthusiastic converts to ideas such as 'managing by walking about' and opening their office doors to the world, but often it was a change without real meaning. There is more to participative management than being able to strike up a conversation with a lathe operator.

People

Tensions between people are part and parcel of any organisation, large or small. Functional organisations have exacerbated this basic fact of life through their belief in specialist knowledge. As we have seen, the functional organisation is based around the creation and rigorous protection of corporate fiefdoms.

In addition to this, tensions between people have been further fuelled in recent years through the development of a more mobile workforce. Young managers can appear to their older colleagues as feckless and untrustworthy, using the organisation as a stepping stone to another career goal.

Values

At the heart of this syndrome of tension are organisational values. Organisations have exhibited a notable tendency to shift their values – to an extent and regularity that they can be rendered entirely meaningless. The poor communication of values and a fundamental lack of consistency creates the strongest tension of all: insecurity. If people in an organisation do not understand or support the values of the organisation then the values are worthless.

Re-engineering attempts to remove functional tensions. It achieves this in a number of ways (see Table 11.2).

Table 11.2

Tension	Action	Energy
Standard inflexible processes	Analysis elimination Clarification	Customer-based Flexible Responsive
Formal systems	Analysis reduction	Informal Flexible
Between new and experienced people	Teamworking	Mutual respect
Between committed and mobile	Clear communication channels Flexible	Mutual support Personal development
Autocratic and participative managers	Reduce hierarchy Collective decision-making	Managerial coherence
Supportive and blaming managers	Teamworking at managerial level	Energy focused
Risk-taking and risk-aversion	Teamworking Clear statement of values Consistency	Backing for risk
Fragmented and integrated values	Statement of values Constant communication of values through action	Direction

2. Contact with customers

In their book, *The Virtual Corporation*,[22] William Davidow and Michael Malone describe the achievements of a large number of organisations in becoming extraordinarily close to customers. So close, in fact, that they can regularly exceed customer expectations. 'The ideal virtual product or service is one that is produced instantaneously and customised in response to customer demand,' they write. The final product or service received by the customer is a summation of all the knowledge, processes and behaviours existing in the organisation. They are all working towards reaching a simultaneous goal when the customer walks through the door.

On a practical level, re-engineering brings more employees into direct contact with customers. Reuters, for example, reduced the number of customers covered by individual employees so that closer and more personal relationships could be developed. Other organisations are making similar strides to bring themselves closer to customers. This can be achieved in a myriad of ways. UK building society Legal & General has introduced customer advisory groups made up of brokers and agents who meet at least every three months. The ideas which emerged from these panels were used to produce a report, 'Commitment to Customer Service', which now forms the heart of the company's quality programme. Part of the report lists 38 processes, including policy quotation, underwriting and claims settlement, and gives the company's performance over the latest and previous quarters.

In *Re-engineering the Corporation*, Hammer and Champy cite the example of the US food chain Taco Bell which was losing customers fast when it decided to ask customers what they actually wanted. Customers wanted good food, served fast, in a clean environment, at a price they could afford. It seems obvious enough, but Taco Bell had got out of the habit of asking and had forgotten that customers aren't interested in the finer points of how all this is achieved. Taco Bell decided to reduce everything except the costs of goods sold. Layers of management were eliminated, nearly every job was re-defined and restaurant managers were given greater responsibility for the way their own restaurant was run. One hundred managers were put on call to solve problems in the company's 2,300 restaurants – previously there had also been 350 area managers controlling 1,800 restaurants. Taco Bell moved from a situation where 70 per cent of the restaurant was kitchen area and 30 per cent was for customers, to the exact reverse, doubling seating in the same building, with takings up substantially.

Q

- How easy is it for customers to contact you directly?
- How does your organisation canvass and act on the ideas of customers?
- How many customers do you meet regularly?
- How many people in your organisation have direct contact with customers?

---

3. Responsibility

Quality gurus Deming and Juran have championed quality as the responsibility of everyone. They argue that if people are given the tools and techniques to check their own work then inspection by quality controllers is all but eliminated and people have a far greater sense of pride in their work. In contrast, Deming argues that leaving responsibility for quality to an inspector at the end of the procedure simply leads to the fault multiplying and linking with others. The result is a costly high percentage of rejected products. In an example, cited by Deming, RCA sought to maximise its profits by using cheaper and inferior parts in its televisions. As a result, more sets broke down while under guarantee and many proved too expensive to repair and had to be discarded and expensively replaced by the company.

Q

- Who handles customer complaints in your organisation?
- How much time do you spend checking the work of others?

Re-engineering at the American insurance company, Aetna Life and Casualty, has granted substantial autonomy to its sales force. The old hierarchy of supervisors and agents has been replaced by work teams of around 17 people. Aetna has completely overhauled the business of issuing a policy. In 1992 it had 22 business centres with a staff of 3,000. It took around 15 days to get a basic policy out of the office. Now, the operation has been reduced to 700 employees in four centres. Customers receive their policies within five days. A single person sitting at a networked PC can perform all the necessary steps to process an application immediately. It is estimated that the new system for issuing policies will save $40 million and improve productivity by 25 per cent.[23]

Re-engineering takes the ideas championed by Deming and others a stage further. It does not regard the responsibility issue as being specifically to do with production or blue-collar workers. Instead, it sees responsibility as an organisation-wide issue. It recognises that managers are often hidebound by a lack of responsibility or a need to refer matters up the hierarchy or to different functions before they take action. Re-engineering gives both employees and managers more responsibility to identify and solve problems. Many companies claim to do this already. Empowerment has been a popular buzz-word in management circles over recent years. In practice, what it usually means is that people are asked to work longer hours to do the work of people who have been made redundant. This is not empowerment; it is exploitation. Central to re-engineering is a genuine delegation of power so that people throughout the organisation become truly empowered.

One of the difficulties in achieving this is that managers often consider themselves to be already empowered. Often they are not. We were struck by the observations of a senior tutor from a business school. She believed the real value of their corporate development programmes lay in the fact that managers were gathered together in an alien environment where they met the company's top management team. She also believed it was perhaps the only opportunity managers had to question important strategies and the overall direction of the business. And yet, these were senior managers who, if asked, would no doubt have considered themselves influential and powerful individuals. There are many other comparatively senior managers who, if they examined their position, would find that they too are circumvented by the company's decision-making process.

Re-engineering is an act of faith. More responsibility brings a reduction in checks and controls. Managers are challenged to find their own solutions to business problems.

Chemical company, Alcoa, is attempting to question everything it does through its Quantum Leap programme launched in 1991. The company's 25 business unit managers have been given the freedom to formulate and implement initiatives to improve performance. Alcoa estimated that the planned changes could add $1 billion to its operating profits and, by the end of 1992, company chairman Paul O'Neil anticipated that Alcoa was on course to reap an extra $2–3 billion. This, by any measure, is a significant pay-back for granting real power to people.

HOW POWERFUL ARE YOU?

- What kind of business decisions do you make alone?
- What decisions do you refer elsewhere for approval?
- Who do you supervise?
- Who supervises you?
- Do you know the long-term goals of your organisation?
- If so, how did you find them out?

WHAT KIND OF POWER IS IMPORTANT TO YOU?

- Freedom to make important decisions without interference.
- Being responsible for a large number of people.
- Having direct access to the chief executive.
- Being able to co-opt people from throughout the company to solve problems.
- Having a role in strategy formulation.

4. Teams

Teamworking, like empowerment, has been pushed to the forefront of managerial minds in the last decade. The two are closely linked. Both, however, have usually been interpreted as a tool of use only on the factory floor or in creative service businesses such as advertising. By and large, managers have been passed by.

Re-engineering seeks to reverse this by introducing teamworking throughout an organisation. Multi-skilled teams become permanently established and involve everyone. Some may involve customers and suppliers. Teamworking is the accepted way of working throughout the re-engineered organisation – not just on the factory floor. (We look at teamworking in greater detail later in the book.)

An example of the level of teamworking involved can be seen at the German company Bosch. At its new plant in Eisenach, eastern Germany, product line teams are given responsibility for the entire process covered by the line from suppliers to clients. People in the line team are broken down into teams of between 10 and 15 people. The factory's rewards policy is tightly linked to team performance and wages include a team premium for the team's performance as well as elements tied to the views of other team members on an individual's performance.[24]

Though teamworking has attracted a great deal of recent attention, it is worth noting that teamworking does not, in itself, bring an organisation closer to customers. Indeed, research by consultant and author, Colin Coulson-Thomas, involving more than 100 organisations, concluded that teamworking was often failing to deliver quality and other performance improvements. 'There is a danger that groups or teams are focusing excessively on internal dynamics at the expense of external customers,' warned Coulson-Thomas.[25] Teams are an essential factor in re-engineering and other change initiatives, but not an all-embracing automatic solution. They, too, can lead to the sort of demarcations which so weaken functional approaches to business organisation.

Q

● Are teams a permanent fixture in your organisation or an *ad hoc* temporary solution to individual projects?

● How many teams are you part of?

● What new skills have you developed to improve your teamworking?

- When things go wrong do you share the blame?
- How much information do you share with people in your team?
- How much information do you share with others in your organisation?
- Do you have a support infrastructure for sharing information?
- How many major decisions in your organisation are joint ones?

5. Flexible work

Teamworking can only be effective if it is supported by flexible attitudes and practice of work. Advanced Engineering Systems (AES), a supplier of parts to Toyota and Honda, employs around 50 people. It is a small company, within which 50 per cent of team members can perform every operation on one 13-machine line; and 60 per cent can perform 80 per cent of the tasks. And the proportions are set to further increase.[26] In the re-engineered organisation jobs are multi-dimensional. This does not only apply to factory-floor workers, but everyone in the organisation.

- At IBM Credit four types of specialist have been replaced by a single, multi-skilled 'deal structurer', who calls a small central pool of specialist back-up staff when needed.
- Microsoft has 15 grades of management. At its top are seven people known as the 'architects'. They involve themselves in any projects which require attention and then evaluate the issues at stake. They are the seven with whom the company's chief executive Bill Gates works, and through whom he communicates his ideas to the rest of the organisation.
- At AT&T multi-functional 'design cells' handle each project from cus-tomer request to delivery. This previously involved specialists in five different departments.
- At Bell Atlantic a 'case team' carries out previously separate tasks.

The requirement for multi-skilled and flexible workers and managers poses important questions for development and training – and for providers of this training. Peter Beddowes, dean of Ashridge Management College, argues that traditional business schools have no place in the new environment of constant change:

> If business schools re-invent themselves as responsive centres of learning, they have a crucial role to play. The characteristics of these centres of learning are: a focus on learning to learn; partnerships; managers as learning facilitators and

learning facilitators as managers; a comprehensive portfolio of resources; professional diagnostics and counselling; networking; a multi-cultural and global perspective; use of IT; relationship marketing and database management; and collaborative organisation.[27]

Managers are no longer able to view the skills of management as a rag-bag of different specialities which they can pick up along the way. Management development will no longer be a question of topping up a particular skill or adding another to your portfolio. Instead, the emphasis will be on managers taking responsibility for their own development. If they are truly empowered to do their job, they also need to be empowered to manage their own development.

Q

- Do you have a clear idea of your job role?
- Do you often refer to your job description?
- If you wrote a description of your role would it match the one you already have?
- Have you identified core skill areas which you need to develop?

FIRST STEPS

1. IDENTIFY YOUR CORPORATE RECIPE

Recognition is the first step towards re-engineering. In the same way as anyone with a compulsive habit has to recognise and admit that he or she has a problem if they are to solve it, organisations have to acknowledge their need to change. This can only be achieved if there is clear understanding of their current corporate recipe.

As we have outlined, managers and organisations are adept at avoiding the harsher truths of reality. Managers often recognise that changes, which the organisation does not fully understand, are afoot in the marketplace. They might recognise that the company employs too many people doing non-essential jobs, but they don't necessarily do anything about it. The *status quo* emerges untouched almost every time. The warning signs that an organisation must change are usually clear – at least, to the objective and unbiased observer not embroiled in the day-to-day life of an organisation. (This is not an advertisement for consultants – they may identify a need for change, but may be totally unable to prepare or persuade the organisation to manage change.)

Fully understanding how your own organisation works, approaches problems and sets about tackling them is never easy. From a business point of view it is worth considering some of the following issues.

Time competitiveness – how quick are you?

- Are decisions made speedily?
- Can you move heaven and earth to get something important done?
- Are you the fastest in the business at converting orders into completed deliveries?
- Are you the fastest in the business at converting ideas into products?

People competitive – have you the right people with the right training?

- Is training handled in an *ad hoc* manner as an occasional indulgence rather than systematically as a commercial necessity?
- Do people take responsibility for their own development?
- Is everyone trained regularly or are senior managers missed out?
- Does the organisation have a clear idea of the competences required of its staff?
- Are your manning levels higher than your competitors?

Cost competitive – how expensive is running your business, now and tomorrow?

- Is cost control regarded as the responsibility of the finance department and no one else?
- Do you have a clear idea of the costs involved in your side of the business?
- Is controlling costs regarded as more important than satisfying customers?

Productivity – is your organisation productive enough?

- Does your organisation have any systematic means of measuring productivity?
- How do your productivity levels compare with those elsewhere in your industry?

● How is productivity going to be enhanced in the future?

Organisations need also to consider how effective they are at meeting the needs of customers and examine their track record at implementing performance improvement initiatives such as TQM (total quality management). Equally valuable insight into the current corporate recipe can be gained from less easily measured sources of information. Consider the following:

What do people tell stories about? An organisation which is dominated by a single function will usually be full of managers circulating stories – often apocryphal – about the excesses of the individual function. If stories circulate about the marketing department importing a herd of elephants so it could get the right photograph for the company's brochure, then there is probably a sense that the marketing department is out of control, governed by different rules from the rest of the organisation. Even if this is not entirely true, the feeling is usually strong enough to create dissatisfaction. So, think about the stories you tell and those you have heard. What do they tell you about the organisation's priorities?

What gets you fired? Companies have different interpretations of what justifies your desk being cleared on the spot. Some may demand your departure if you overspend on your budget, while others may regard questioning the chief executive's strategic thinking as a heinous corporate crime. Again, a company's judgement of what is important is helpful in determining what kind of organisation it is. As an adjunct to this, consider what rules are thought to be sacrosanct, the breaking of which gets people into deep trouble.

How do you get promoted? This seems straightforward, but in different organisations different skills, behaviour and performance will lead to your personal success. In some companies working hard and keeping quiet are as likely to lead to success as a habit of questioning the judgement of senior managers.

Coming to terms with your own organisation is often called an *organisational audit*. We believe this is too ornate and formal a term for the process. The 'soft' elements of a company's culture and behaviour are as likely to be established by the kind of gossip doing the rounds and how people usually succeed in the organisation. An organisational audit is a grand name for a simple task. It involves examining how you and your organisation works.

People do tend, however, to be more comfortable in the first place with a more formal approach. A conventional organisational audit should cover six areas:

- what people do;
- how performance is measured and rewarded;
- how the organisation is structured;
- how the organisation uses IT;
- what values drive the organisation;
- what skills do the organisation's people have and require.

How you view the world

Considering all of these questions should give you some idea of the constraints under which you and your organisation now work. The next step in looking at your existing corporate recipe is to think of how your organisation views the world. Which one of the four categories below best sums up your organisation's view?

1. We need to do more of the same in slightly different conditions.
2. We know where to go but don't know how.
3. We know where to go but getting there looks demanding.
4. We don't know where to go but realise we can't stay here.

The companies which have the most chance of making re-engineering happen are likely to come from the fourth group. They are uninhibited by the pessimism evident in the third outlook, or the blind confidence of the first two. They are, perhaps, aware of the organisational truism: 'The minute you establish an organisation it starts to decay'. The challenge for managers is to persuade people throughout the organisation that it simply cannot continue to operate in its traditional way. It must change.

The trouble for many managers is that they are part and parcel of the existing culture. Indeed, they may well have played an important role in its creation. They have to prove that they have changed in as persuasive a manner as possible. This explains why fundamental changes often require a new top management team, one unconnected with the existing recipe. A new chief executive, management team or a take-over is often the jump start an organisation requires. Typically, the re-engineering programme at the building society N&P began with the arrival of a new chief executive.

While a new management team often makes the process easier, it is not essential. This is how one managing director showed his organisation that he had changed. His conversion occurred when he looked at other organisations his company dealt with.

> They were actually making our job harder and, often, creating confusion. I saw that their problems were rooted in the fact that different parts of their organisations often failed to communicate with each other as well as those they dealt with externally. I then looked at the way we were organised. I knew divisions existed and people worked in their own compartments. But, as I looked closer, I saw that we had our own functional silos. There weren't any walls of stone, but there was a failure to communicate or share ideas. People were often unwilling to take responsibility for their actions. They would simply blame another department.

The managing director realised that he too had benefitted from the functional silos – indeed, he took some responsibility for their creation. 'I have worked my way up through the company and I'm sure that I have actually used and created silos to take a step forward. It is part of what was once a permissible technique of management: divide and conquer.' The first stage in breaking down the invisible but historical barriers was to call 60 of the 7,000 workforce together and explain the concept. What the managing director was doing, through his candour about his own responsibility, was bringing the unspoken into the open. 'If you admit it, you are encouraging people to change,' he says. 'The key thing was that people recognised the silos.'

If, at first, you don't succeed there are a number of ruses which may be of use. Humour can be helpful. If you continually ridicule the existing recipe, seeds of doubt will quickly spread throughout the organisation. Additionally, a manager can put feedback into the system. If a customer comments that deliveries are slow and unreliable, it is worth making sure that this information gains maximum publicity rather than being swept under the carpet. Perhaps the most common approach is to introduce impossibly hard criteria measures. You may realise, for example, that the product development process is far too long. For the next product, gather the team together and tell them that you want the new product in half the time. They will shake their heads in disbelief. If you insist that that is what you want they will be forced to go back and try to figure out how they can do it. Some will realise that their existing way of working restrains their performance; the recipe is holding them back. One insurance company set a target of processing all customer transactions within 24 hours – at the time the process took several months.

2. IDENTIFY YOUR GOALS AND NECESSARY CONDITIONS

Having identified how your organisation thinks and behaves, the next step is to consider how you would like it to to think and behave, and to consider its organisational goal and necessary conditions, the basics it needs to achieve to stay in business.

What is your goal? In Lewis Carroll's *Alice's Adventures in Wonderland*, there is a poignant piece of dialogue: ' "Would you tell me, please, which way I ought to go from here?" she asked. "That depends a good deal on where you want to get to," said the cat.'

Goals may well be multi-faceted and organisations certainly exist in a more complex and competitive environment than ever before, but any organisation should be able to condense its goals into a single pithy statement. This should be accessible, motivational and realistic. It should not be jargon-filled and incomprehensible to most people, nor ridiculously idealistic, nor matter of fact.

What are your necessary conditions? These are the basics for continuing survival. For commercial organisations the most obvious are profitability and money (cash-flow). They also include legislative and regulatory standards to which your organisation has to conform.

3. THE 'STICKY STEPS' APPROACH TO PLANNING

Armed with your organisational goal and aware of your necessary conditions for continuing existence, you have somewhere to go, however distant and unfocused this may seem. In the traditional paradigm, the next step would be to delegate the task of moving the process forward to the planning department. Planning has become elevated to a precise, statistics-driven, corporate art. But, the true nature of planning is continuously to gain and maintain perspective. In addition, you require co-ordination to spread and to use the perspective among stakeholders in the business. The two things are separate. This has to be recognised by any organisation seeking to implement change.

Planning has nothing to do with time schedules and bar charts. These simply represent the ways in which we communicate the plan to our stakeholders. Planning can be little more than the process of gaining and maintaining perspective. If accomplished change is change chosen carefully, then we need methods to help us to choose our change successfully. Imagine you are at the end of a long journey in which your project has been completed. Look back at it and describe what you did. This approach, which we label 'sticky steps', allows you to look backwards, going from a complete and Herculean task, which is almost too large to contemplate, to tiny little steps which you could wake up on Monday and do. All you need to complete this exercise is a large number of the now ubiquitous post-it notes.

Sticky Steps[28]

Step one – work out the 'what' of your project; what it is you want to achieve.

Step two – write on a large sheet of paper, 'In order to have . . .'.

Step three – write down the 'what' on a post-it note. Start with a verb in the past tense. For example, 'Installed re-engineering'.

In order to have . . .   installed re-engineering

Step four – continue with the sentence you have written on the large sheet. Write, 'We would have had to have . . .'.

Step five – imagine that you have actually completed the project and you are looking backwards in time. Write on a post-it note anything you can imagine you would have had to have done.

Step six – place the post-it note on the board underneath the sentence to the right-hand side.

Step seven – ask yourself, is there anything else?

Step eight – if there is, write it down on another post-it note.

Step nine – go back to *Step seven* until there is nothing further to add.

In order to have . . .		installed re-engineering	
We would have had to have . . .			
Found out which processes we have and which are good and bad	Brought my boss up to speed	Brought my colleagues up to speed	Followed through the business to establish the chains of activities we routinely carry out

Step ten – choose one of the stickers and use it to replace the original 'what' (at the end of 'In order to have . . .'). Place the original 'what' in the top right-hand corner of the board.

Step eleven – now move all the other yellow stickers to the left-hand side of the board.

Step twelve – go back to *Step five*.

Step thirteen – repeat this loop until the stickers have tasks written on them. That is, things you could wake up on Monday morning and decide you were going to do and then get on with doing them.

Step fourteen – move the tasks to the top right-hand corner of the board.

Step fifteen – discard all the stickers you generated in the loop getting to the tasks.

Step sixteen – take the next sticker from the bottom left-hand side.

Step seventeen – go back to *Step five*.

Step eighteen – when you have worked your way through all the loops the first part of the process is over.

KEY POINTS

1. Identify your corporate recipe – look at hard and soft criteria.
2. Identify your goals and necessary conditions.
3. Use the 'sticky steps' approach to planning.

Notes

1 Pascale, R, quoted in 'Turning doers back into thinkers', *Independent on Sunday*, 28 November 1993.
2 *Passenger Car Distribution Trends to 2000*, Economist Intelligence Unit, 1992.
3 Sadler, P, *Managing Talent*, FT/Pitman Publishing, London, 1993.
4 Ashridge Management Research Group, *Triggers for Change*, AMRG, 1989.
5 Crainer, S & Clutterbuck, D, *Makers of Management*, Macmillan, London, 1990.
6 Crainer, S & Clutterbuck, D, *Makers of Management*, Macmillan, London, 1990.
7 Simon, H, *Administrative Behaviour*, Macmillan, New York, 1947.
8 Obeng, E, Kirkbride, P & Durcan, J, 'The revolutionary reality of change', *Directions*, September 1993.
9 Devine, M, 'Radical re-engineering', *Directions*, September 1993.
10 Mintzberg, H & Westley, F, 'Cycles of organizational change', *Strategic Management Journal*, Vol. 13, 1992.
11 Beckard, R, *Organization Development: Strategies and Models*, Addison-Wesley, Reading, Mass., 1969.
12 Trapp, R, 'How to ride the winds of change', *Independent on Sunday*, 12 December 1993.
13 KPMG, *Change Management*, KPMG, 1993.
14 Massarik, F, 'Chaos and change: examining the aesthetics of organisation development', in *Advances in Organization Development*, Vol. 1, Ablex, New Jersey, 1990.
15 Champy, J, & Hammer, M, *Reengineering the Corporation*, Nicholas Brealey, London, 1993.
16 Lorenz, C, 'Change is not enough', *Financial Times*, 12 January 1994.
17 Morgan, G, *Imaginization*, Sage Publications, London, 1993.
18 Bleeke, J & Ernst, D, *Collaborating to Compete*, John Wiley, New York, 1993.
19 Lorenz, C, 'Quantum leaps in a dangerous game', *Financial Times*, 22 September 1993.
20 Lorenz, C, 'Restoring order from chaos', *Financial Times*, 2 June 1993.
21 Trapp, R, 'How to ride the winds of change', *Independent on Sunday*, 12 December 1993.
22 Davidow, W & Malone, M, *The Virtual Corporation*, HarperCollins, New York, 1992.
23 *'The technology pay-off'*, *Business Week*, 14 June 1993.
24 Eisenhammer, J, 'Breaking old moulds through competition', *Independent on Sunday*, 19 December 1993.
25 Coulson-Thomas, C, *Harnessing the Potential of Groups*, Lotus Development, 1993.
26 Griffiths, J, 'Driving out the old regime', *Financial Times*, 20 August 1993.
27 Beddowes, P, 'Reinventing management development', *Directions*, December 1993.
28 Sticky Steps, copyright © EDA Obeng 1994.

2

MOVING FROM FUNCTIONS TO PROCESSES

WHAT ARE PROCESSES?

'It is not products, but the processes that create products that bring companies long-term success. Good products don't make winners; winners make good products,' say James Champy and Michael Hammer in *Re-engineering the Corporation*.[1] If a company divides itself along product lines few eyebrows are raised. A building society, for example, divided its operations into separate businesses in the 1980s. These included mortgages, life policies and credit cards. Though it appears to be a logical thing to do, the trouble is that the fascination with products overlooks customers who are not so easily separated. A single customer may take out a mortgage and a life policy and want another credit card. They would prefer to be able to do so from a single entity rather than being passed from one product division to another.

The faith in good products leading to competitiveness is long-established. Yet, time and time again innovative products have failed to yield the anticipated financial results. Other companies quickly copy them or produce their own versions of the product. With time-cycles diminishing this is more efficiently done than ever before. Organisations can no longer rely on a new product reaping huge dividends over a lengthy period as competitors try to make up the lost ground. Products are now easily copied and retain their uniqueness for a shorter and shorter time.

In contrast, processes are more robust competitive weapons. They are unique to a particular organisation and, as such, are virtually impossible to copy. The trouble is that understanding and utilising that uniqueness is not easy. While processes, not products, lie at the heart of re-engineering, their identification and mapping is perhaps the most controversial aspect of the entire transformation. Understanding processes fully is time-consuming, complex and involves negotiating the maze of corporate politics and functional strongholds. It involves finding out who does what, where, why and with what impact on the organisation's main constituencies. If you think about a task which forms an important part of your work you will quickly see what a minefield process analysis is. Consider a few basic questions:

- Why do you do the task?
- Where do you do it?
- When and for how long?
- Who else is involved in completing the task?
- Whom does the task affect inside your organisation?
- Whom does the task affect outside the organisation?
- What resources do you use to complete the task?
- What information do you need to complete the task?

Any task you do can be looked at in terms of time, people, resources, information, internal users and external users. And, in addition, there is always a hefty dose of personal relationships, politics and sensitivities.

Complex though process analysis clearly is, at its heart is a straightforward idea. A process has been defined as 'any activity, or group of activities, that takes an input, adds value to it, and provides an output to an internal or external customer'.[2] Alternatively, a process can be seen as a group of activities which cause change to happen through the execution of a number of simultaneous tasks. The change and the processes are in line with the organisation's goals and aligned, as closely as possible, to the needs of an organisation's core constituencies.

There is nothing mysterious or startlingly original about processes. All organisations have processes and they are a concept which people easily understand. The trouble is that people may not recognise the fact that their activities form part of a process. To convince people that they really do understand what a process is, give them the following list of tasks and ask them to arrange the tasks in order (post-it notes are, yet again, ideal for this exercise):

● PREPARE SEED BED	● PLANT PLANTS
● CHECK BUDGET	● GO TO NURSERY
● DIG THEM UP AGAIN	● WEED AND LOOK AFTER
● CHOOSE STYLE OF BED	PLANTS
	● CHOOSE PLANTS

What emerges is an outline of a process. It is sequential though, in practice, once implemented it will be simultaneous. Though people will have different ideas as to the order in which the tasks should be handled, it is nevertheless a process.

Re-engineering does not look at processes from a narrow or functional perspective. Instead, it looks across an industry – from supplier to customer – to identify those factors that influence how well the company sells, delivers, produces and services its market. Subsequently, it takes the view of each individual stakeholder and seeks to remove steps, activities, sub-processes and sometimes whole departments which do not play an essential part in the process. In some instances, it is worth remembering that companies often actually take a wider view and look beyond their direct customer to the customer's customer – a company like Heinz, for example, has to look beyond its customer (the retail chain or wholesaler) to the customer's customer (the shopper).

Of course, companies and their managers will say that they already have long-standing and efficient processes which are in tune with the needs of customers and end-users. Some do, but they are usually confined to a small aspect of the business or a single function. There may, for example, be a clearly defined process for invoicing. More often, processes have become over-wieldy, their overall point and objective lost in the murk of corporate history. With time processes tend to become biased towards particular resources and individual processes are regarded as 'important'; they become recipe rather than business-oriented.

The way companies develop strategy is a good example of what has happened to many processes. The process of strategy formulation and implementation has become highly complex. Companies employ managers specifically to develop comprehensive strategic plans. The trouble is that though these documents are often presented in a persuasive format, they can bear little relation to reality. Strategy has become a function and strategists, consumed by a narrow functional-based outlook, have become distanced from the customer. Instead of creating strategies which are based around anticipated customer and market needs, they produce documents notable for their exhaustive detail, covering every possible scenario. In fact, the task and the process to achieve the task have become submerged and largely forgotten. What emerges is a document which has a life of its own and then dies a slow death on the shelves of managers who regard it as an impediment, rather than an invitation, to action.

A similar affliction has struck other apparently simple processes. As an example take what happened at a top international hotel in Paris. The

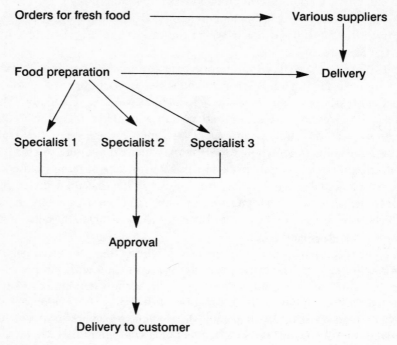

Figure 12.1

management identified a major problem in its restaurant and kitchen service. Revenue was down, quality was inconsistent, service poor, traditional demarcations in place and morale diminishing. The process of satisfying customers in the restaurant was straightforward enough (see Figure 12.1). What should have been a simple process was complicated by a number of factors: orders were made continuously throughout the day; there were a large number of specialist suppliers; deliveries arrived at no specific time; jobs in the kitchen were specialised and strong demarcations existed; as a result of the time-consuming nature of the process the chefs had little time for planning menus to make the most effective use of resources and which were appealing and tasty. The hotel's food preparation process was a classic 'A' shape with all the activities being brought together at the last moment to provide a product (see Figure 12.2). This is an approach common throughout much of manufacturing industry, and elsewhere.

After carefully examining the food preparation process, the hotel completely re-designed its kitchen operations and restaurant area. The process was revolutionised. Instead of ordering a range of fresh foodstuffs from a

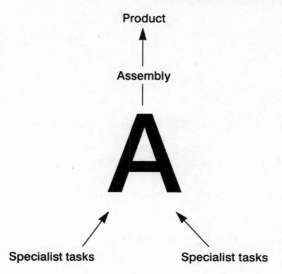

Figure 12.2

large number of suppliers, the hotel ordered pre-prepared food – salads, sauces and sweets – from a single source which also provided supplies like meat and fish which could not be pre-prepared. This meant that less kitchen staff were needed to prepare meals. The remaining staff took on a wider range of responsibilities – motivated by the fact that much of their previously mundane work had effectively been removed. With less room required for storage, the hotel was able to reduce the size of its kitchen and increase restaurant space. The hotel had realised that customers didn't actually care who prepared their salad or where it was done, so long as it was tasty and fresh. This realisation changed the production process's shape from an 'A' to a 'T' with the individual tailoring of the product being left to the last moment (see Figure 12.3).

As with the food preparation example, the outcome of many process analyses is that the tasks of a number of functions become merged. Instead of operating around functions and divisions that have been made for the convenience of managers and which often obscure the customer, re-engineered companies try to identify precisely every decision, action and task that ultimately contributes to the final product or service. These activities come together to form a process, such as order fulfilment or product realisation, and typically flow through the organisation, cutting across different departments and functions.

Defining these core processes allows business leaders to take a more

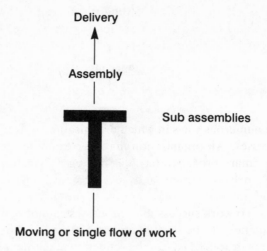

Figure 12.3

rigorous, systematic approach to the critical processes that satisfy customer needs. Instead of measuring the performance of individual functions and then hoping that this will add up to an improved product or service, measuring processes enable companies to know precisely how well they are performing in the external market. They can take a core process, identify the inputs and outputs of that process and then measure key performance indicators, such as how long it takes to deliver the output and at what cost and quality.

Re-engineering takes a company and customer-wide view of processes rather than seeing them in isolation. The emphasis is on integration. In contrast, many of the most popular management concepts of recent years have tackled small numbers of processes or taken a narrow perspective. In fact, re-engineering takes ideas such as JIT and TQM, the learning organisation, lean production, competing in time, the supplier/customer chain, process-based costing and customer-oriented production, and seeks to unify and integrate them so that they work coherently and consistently to add value to the customer's experience both inside and outside the organisation.

Process-based management enables large, complex international companies to ensure that crucial processes do not become fragmented across different divisions. Exxon Chemical International has, for example, identified a common process for its customer supply chain. It constitutes supply/demand, order commitment, finished product inventory, despatch and delivery, and procurement of third-party services (which account for half of the supply chain costs). The end-result, predicts Jim Harris, president of Exxon Chemical, is that 'a common process will be the norm. Any deviation from that rule will have to justify itself in added value terms'.[3]

WHAT TYPES OF PROCESSES ARE THERE?

There are numerous ways in which organisations can separate and identify their processes. An organisation may, for example, draw a simple divide between primary processes (such as buying raw materials) and secondary processes (such as training and development). The trouble is that after identifying processes, organisations often adhere too rigidly to their definitions. To work successfully, processes cannot be written in tablets of stone. They need to be flexible and responsive. If the needs of customers change, then processes have to be refined to meet them.

Though re-engineering centres on the identification and clarification of processes, there are a great many dangers attached to this. The main one is inflexibility. Take this example of how a textile company manufactures its products. The process runs:

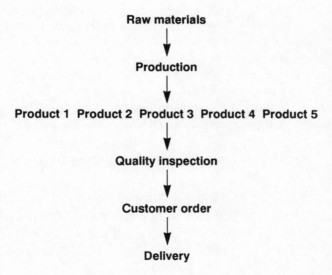

Raw materials

Production

Product 1   Product 2   Product 3   Product 4   Product 5

Quality inspection

Customer order

Delivery

This process seem logical enough. Its weakness, however, lies in the fact that the products are customised at the beginning of the process. The company is often left with large amounts of a particular coloured material. One solution to this is for the organisation to customise its products at a far later stage, leaving its options open so that it can manufacture what customers have already stated a preference for rather than what the company imagines they have a preference for.

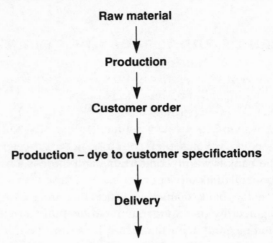

Raw material

Production

Customer order

Production – dye to customer specifications

Delivery

In many organisations processes are interpreted as neat and tidy theoretical exercises. You can sit down and draw up a process which looks logical and effective on paper. You can then hand it to the people you think should implement it and walk away. The trouble is that processes are not as clinically scientific as many managers would like. They involve high-quality people and project management skills.

The attraction of processes is that by mapping them organisations can establish the key processes on which they need to focus. Organisations can identify the constraints and obstacles preventing them reaching their goals; processes provide a common map and language for the organisation so that companies can identify missing links and areas of repetition or needless work; and processes provide an important starting point for re-designing an organisation's activities.

It is helpful to make a comparison with engineering which is based around six basic processes: reaction; separation; aggregation; homogenisation; transfer; and storage. In management terms, if you categorise various processes in a similar way a number of steps are found – we have labelled these unit operations:

- *Transformation* – action on a particular task or project which leads to a change in character or culture.
- *Identification* – separating customers or markets into smaller, more clearly defined, units.

- *Unification* – bringing groups of customers or markets together.
- *Consistency* – creating uniformity of output or input.
- *Movement* – moving groups from one section or part of the process to another.
- *Holding* – the waiting period when customers are maintained in a controlled environment.
- *Offering* – the end-result or output as experienced by the consumer.

There are a variety of ways in which each stage could be handled. Take the example of opening an account at a bank. The stages in this process are:

- Holding – you wait in the bank for your appointment with the bank manager. The bank has made great efforts to make this a pleasant experience. The bank is warm, comfortable and there is a wide range of information about all of its services.
- Unification – in the bank manager's office the process of unification begins. The manager wants to understand your needs as a customer and does so by meeting you face-to-face and by fitting your needs into a specific product offered by the bank.
- Transformation – the bank manager runs a credit check, converting available information into a decision.
- Unification – the bank manager gathers together a wide range of details about your status and financial situation.
- Transformation – the bank manager offers you a new account. You are now, officially, a customer.
- Movement – you wait in the manager's office as he or she goes to the front desk to sort out your account number and a temporary cheque book.
- Offering – the manager returns, gives you all the documentation and you leave.

In clean-sheet design it is often easiest to design using the unit operations before plunging into what actually occurs in the unit operation. For example, an airline might choose to have an overall process which runs:

- unification;
- holding;
- movement;
- holding;
- offering.

It may, however, look at different ways of holding – in a Club Lounge, in the main foyer; movement could be by coach, car or travolator, and so on.

WORKING WITH CUSTOMERS AND SUPPLIERS

Re-engineering begins its analysis of processes with the end-user – the customer, client, consumer or other constituency. To do so there must be an understanding of the end-users' needs and aspirations. It is worth remembering some important differences:

A **customer** is an individual or organisation which exchanges money for the offer provided by the organisation. The customer *may* be invited by the organisation to drive the output of the process or the process itself.

A **consumer** is an individual or organisation after which the process comes to an end. They do not pass on the **offering** in any shape or form. The client or customer may often be the consumer.

A **client** is an individual or organisation wanting to use the output of the process – the **offering** – or the individual or organisation which wants to use the output of the project – the **deliverables**. The term 'client' tends to describe an individual or organisation with a mutually agreed role that they drive at least the output of the process and sometimes the process itself.

The interweaving of clients, customers, consumers and other end-users is symptomatic of the growing complexity of relationships between organisations and those who buy and use their products and services. Parallel to this is the increasingly complex nature of customer demand for both consumer and industrial goods. Consider the case of a retail chain which seeks to co-ordinate the activities of promotion, manufacture, warehousing, logistics, procurement, supply and direct product pricing from its suppliers. Functional approaches which serially process the customer through these activities are inappropriate as the nature of the demand is simultaneous.

Quality in respect to customer service is critical to effective business processes. Abrupt changes in the business environment often mean that incremental change is insufficient. Re-engineering simultaneously aims to improve service standards and lower costs. Quality guru JM Juran believes that 80 per cent of problems encountered in organisations can be put down to systems and the remaining 20 per cent to people. Re-engineering seeks to create truly customer-oriented systems run by people who fully understand the processes they are involved in and who are trained to carry out many different tasks within the process.

Implicit to re-engineering is a recognition that the age of customers taking charge has arrived. Mass production is giving way to mass customisation. In the early part of the century, Henry Ford was quite content to produce a car in a single colour. Variation was expensive. Ford kept it simple and once observed, 'I've got no use for a motor that has more spark plugs than a cow has teats'. Now, customers demand much more. When US aircraft maker Boeing asked its customers what they would like in the new Boeing 777, they requested that it should have galleys and toilets which could be relocated anywhere in the cabin within hours. In May 1995 when the first Boeing 777 is produced the owners will be able to re-arrange the aircraft within hours, configuring it with one, two or three passenger classes to fit the market at the time.[4]

The development of the 777 is an excellent example of an organisation being forced, through the growing competitiveness of its markets, to make basic changes in its approach. When it began developing the 777, Boeing recognised that it was lagging behind its competitors. McDonnell Douglas and Airbus had a substantial head start. 'We knew how to build aircraft but not how to operate them. We had to learn how to think like an airline,' says Boeing's Ron Ostrowski. Boeing radically altered its product design process. Instead of performing design and development tasks sequentially, it began running them in parallel. Functions were displaced by design teams which also included customers. Ideas from a British Airways team, for example, helped the Boeing designers install an extra 12 seats, making the 777 more attractive to potential customers.[5]

Customers want involvement and choice, and they want the latest technology can give. Therefore, companies have to change their offerings quickly and frequently. Customers demand products which meet their needs, delivery when they want it and easy payment arrangements. This means people who can make operational decisions well down the line, people who do not mindlessly carry out repetitive processes or give standard answers or exhibitions of helplessness when facing customer queries.

Q

- Can customers contact you easily?

- Do they actually do so?

- How quickly can you respond if a customer wants more information and help?

- Do you regard customers as individual people?

- How do you treat them as individuals?

The obvious corollary of re-engineering processes internally is to move on to external processes, in particular with customers and suppliers. As re-engineering revolves around customer needs this is not really a bolt on to the overall re-engineering process but an integral part of it. Processes do not stop at the factory gate, but revolve around continuous relationships and links with core constituencies wherever they may be.

Most companies assume that they know what their customers want. Few bother to ask more than the most basic questions about customer satisfaction. If and when they do they are often surprised – customers frequently have a unique and detailed insight into how their supplier works and organises itself. Suppliers, too, are similarly neglected. It is increasingly recognised that organisations are missing a major opportunity – it has been estimated that companies spend around 50 per cent of total production costs on suppliers. The Chartered Institute of Purchasing and Supply estimates that some businesses could be spending up to a third more than necessary on suppliers. South London plastics company Hunter Plastics found that its customers emphasised service and profits rather than, as Hunter assumed, price and quality. The market research prompted Hunter to develop closer relationships with its customers. Buyers from customers' organisations have subsequently visited the company's factory to discuss issues that concern them and products have been developed to meet their requirements more accurately and consistently. The end-result is that Hunter Plastics is now the single source of supply for some customers in particular product ranges.

The entire process of building closer relationships between customers and suppliers has become known as partnership sourcing. Its origins lie in large multinationals buying supplies from smaller companies. Companies like Glaxo, Kodak, IBM, Nissan and British Airways, for example, are all champions of the approach. Computer company ICL has nearly 200 suppliers signed to its vendor accreditation scheme. The programme arose from analysis which showed that of 6,500 suppliers, ICL did 70 per cent of its business with a mere 200. Suppliers in the accreditation programme have to achieve high quality standards and are subject to performance evaluations by ICL. They are also expected to link up directly with ICL's electronic trading system and, increasingly, to deliver components directly to the production line. ICL's relationships are such that it shares research and development and formulates joint marketing strategies with its leading software supplier.

As in so many instances, Japan is a rich source of best practice. Toyota, for example, manufactures only a third of its needs in-house. It calls on 300 contractors who are at the top level of its tiered supplier structure and who work closely with Toyota. They are also members of its product development teams. The top tier of suppliers then contract out a lot of the work to smaller suppliers. All the way down the supplier chain, companies are linked by their recognition that working together is a situation which benefits all sides.

A 1993 survey of 280 of the leading European companies by consultants Booz, Allen & Hamilton found that 60 per cent of those interviewed insist on a regular presence at their suppliers, compared with 40 per cent five years previously. The consultants anticipate the figure will soon rise to 75 per cent. In addition to this, companies are reducing their supplier base at more than three per cent a year, a figure which Booz anticipates will double. British Airways, for example, had 10,000 significant suppliers in the 1980s – a figure which has now been reduced to 3,500 and is set to fall further. Booz's research suggested that the best-performing companies are those moving to 'lifetime' agreements or long-term contracts with suppliers. Interestingly, the best also appear to make the most of fewer resources. In many cases the smaller the purchasing department, the more impressive the performance in terms of material costs, material quality and inventory turnover.[6]

The attractions of partnership sourcing are persuasive:

- Adversarial relationships between buyers and suppliers are replaced by ones of mutual support and benefit.
- Large companies can keep costs down by committing themselves to buying greater amounts from smaller suppliers.
- The customer–supplier relationship can be one of mutual learning with both sides benefiting from an external and new perspective on their business.
- Product development is more likely to match customer needs if the customer's business is more fully understood by the supplier.
- Product development is likely to be faster.

It is also worth noting that partnerships are more likely to prosper between organisations which have shaken off narrow functional approaches. An organisation which finds it difficult to communicate quickly and effectively internally is unlikely to be able to manage a successful relationship with an outside organisation of any sort, especially one that can seem, to the traditionally minded, intrusive.

'In a partnership it is unlikely that both parties will have equivalent power,' says Roger Pudney of Ashridge Management College, who has carried out extensive research into customer–supplier partnerships across the world. 'But, both parties should be bringing something very distinct to the relationship which the other partner needs. Traditional adversarial-type relationships lead companies to exercise their power to gain advantage over their competitors, suppliers and customers; in more collaborative relationships this attitude has to be put to one side.'[7]

There are also commercial risks to partnership sourcing. Sharing information, for example, requires high levels of mutual trust. Companies reliant on a single supplier run the risk of their supplier going out of business or attempting to take advantage of the relationship by increasing prices to unacceptable levels.

With rising competitive pressures, it is likely that partnership sourcing will become more widely practised. We believe that organisations which overlook its possibilities when they are re-appraising their processes and structures are missing an opportunity to share valuable knowledge and learning.

NEXT STEPS

At the end of the previous section you should have come to some sort of recognition of your organisation's recipe; the goal of the business and the necessary conditions for it to exist. None of these are permanent fixtures – all do, and must, change. Now, we move on to consider the role of processes in achieving the organisational goal and fulfilling the necessary conditions.

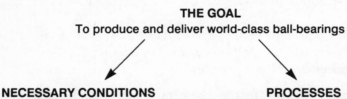

THE GOAL
To produce and deliver world-class ball-bearings

NECESSARY CONDITIONS
Profits and cash
Regulatory requirements

PROCESSES
A set of simultaneous activities whose outcome is measurable as contributing towards the goal or necessary conditions

1. WHAT ARE THE PROCESSES IN YOUR BUSINESS?

The trouble is where to start. Actually identifying core business processes can be one of the most difficult tasks to tackle. Managers don't know the right questions to ask until they have identified the processes they wish to re-engineer. In addition, the trouble with processes is that they can be placed in a variety of contexts. Departmental processes, for example, can be further segmented into process activities, tasks and steps.

In manufacturing companies work flow is often comparatively straightforward to analyse (though changing it is unlikely to be). In service organisations, however, it is highly complex and core processes often prove very elusive. At Rank Xerox UK, the company broke down its activities into 150 sub-processes. It then tried to match up all their inputs and outputs to get a picture of how the whole operated. Discovering who did what and where took six months of debate.

Banca di America e di Italia (BAI) managed to break down its retail banking activities into ten categories, or what it labelled 'families'. These were payments, deposits, withdrawals, money orders, bills, consumer credit, foreign exchange, credit cards, sourcing and end-of-the-day branch processes. Within each family, individual processes were laboriously mapped and then re-designed. The cheque deposit transaction, for example, was broken down from 64 activities, 9 forms and 14 accounts to 25, 2 and 2 respectively. This information was then passed on to BAI's IT team which was charged with making the processes happen.[8]

In reality, it is extremely difficult for any organisation to understand its own processes. Part of the reason for this is that the flow of people, information and materials is often invisible. But, given a great deal of time and energy, the myriad of processes within an organisation can be distilled to a smaller number of core processes. Working on a re-engineering programme at Ashridge Management College, we identified the following core processes:

Primary processes

1A. Client Process – the activities the college carries out with organisations which use its tailored and open services.
1B. Consumer Process – describes the steps experienced by people passing through the college's delivery system.
1C. Customer Processes – all the activities the college carries out with organisations which use its courses and facilities.
1D. Money Collection Process – all the activities for the collection of money from clients, customers and staff.
1E. Products Process – all the ways in which new products are offered to the market and existing products are upgraded.

1F. Market Information Process – the ways in which the market learns of the college's offerings and the college learns of competitive offerings and market demands.

2A. Operations Expenses Payment Process – all processes designed to pay for the cost of generating throughput.

Secondary processes

3. Delivery Preparation Process – all the activities leading to and during service delivery.
4. Resource Planning Process – all the activities designed to give the college control over its future – use of resources of people, facilities and information.
5. Management Process – the ways in which the college synchronises its activities and generates improvements by identifying issues which get in the way of the goals; making the best use of resources to achieve the goal; ensuring all activities are co-ordinated and focused in line with strategy; securing the motivation of the college's people to work towards eliminating the issues which get in the way of achieving the goal.
6. Staff Development Process – the ways in which staff are developed, including recruitment, selection and de-recruitment.
7. Product Mix Decision Process – the ways in which the college decides which offerings to provide.
8. Investment Process – all the ways in which the college decides how the money collected is invested.
9. Strategic Management Process – the ways in which the college identifies future constraints by securing the enthusiasm of employees and commitment and analysing 'what if' scenarios.

Having identified the main processes the problems are only beginning. You quickly realise that there is nothing clear-cut about these processes. They are not definitive and unchanging. Yes, you can identify a small number of processes which drive an organisation's activities, but all appear to be bound up together – here, the image of the writhing mass of snakes is entirely accurate. You will also quickly discover that in any organisation there will be core processes which are not formally recognised or do not exist other than in an *ad hoc* fashion: they happen, but there is no structure to their happening. The links between the processes are also unlikely to be formally recognised or managed. And yet it is obvious that all are tightly linked. Look at how the processes at Ashridge are linked (see Figure 12.4).

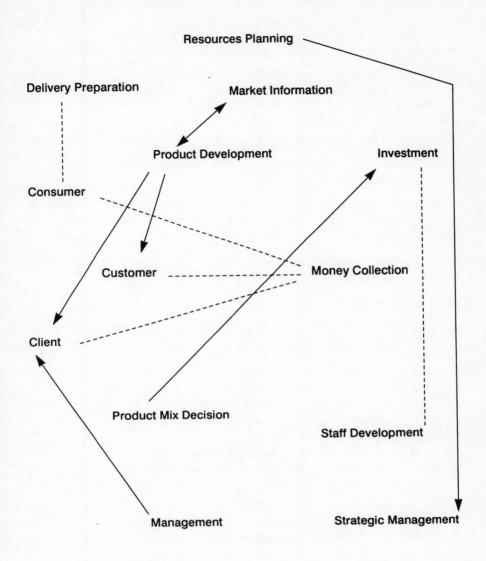

Figure 12.4

2. WHO ARE YOUR KEY CONSTITUENCIES?

At this stage it is easy to overlook the entire point of identifying processes. They appear complex already – and you haven't even considered the core constituencies of the business or whether they actually help the organisation fulfil its goal. If you are to take a broader and more effective view of processes you must first identify the core stakeholders whose satisfaction is paramount to your continuing commercial success.

Customers, Clients and Consumers – are the processes truly geared to their needs? To what extent is their input collected and implemented to make the processes better service their needs?

Employees – are the human resources of the organisation put to the best possible use, or is there a great deal of wasteful duplication of roles and responsibilities?

Owners – which processes are of interest to the organisation's owners and how do the owners have an input into them?

Regulators – which processes involve regulatory bodies?

Suppliers – how are suppliers involved in the processes and would greater involvement from them make the processes more efficient?

Q

- What do your customers expect from your organisation?
- Do you consistently deliver what they want?
- How do you know?
- What do your employees expect and receive from the organisation?
- What do your suppliers expect and receive from the organisation?

---

3. MAKE PROCESSES VISIBLE

Clearly, there are some processes which fail to contribute effectively to your organisational goal, necessary conditions or the needs of core constituents. They either need to be eliminated entirely or examined so that the cause of the inefficiency is identified. If you have identified a problem area within the central processes, you can then concentrate on breaking the process down into the tasks which make it up, the inputs of information, people and resources. Mapping individual processes involves a great deal of complexity, but, in making processes visible, it becomes easier to identify where things are going wrong; you can identify which resources are required, which people need to be involved and where there are grey areas between functions and individuals.

Figure 12.5 is an example of a business process map covering all the steps from a client visiting an organisation to a proposal being sent out. By making a process visible in this way it becomes possible to identify who should contribute to the process, at what stage and with what resources. It is also possible to see where the current system is ill-equipped to allow the process to run smoothly.

4. CREATE A PROCESS VISION

Once you have identified the core processes it is a good idea to bring groups together to discuss and brainstorm the main issues involved in each process. The groups should cover the entire organisation rather than individual functions. It is worth remembering that people always think the processes relating to someone else's job are far simpler than those they have to deal with in their own work. You should involve people who might make use of the outcome of the processes (such as customers) and people who perform the current processes. The aim should be to find out what's possible, what isn't, current difficulties, constraints and ideas. You need their ideas on what they think they need in the future to do their jobs more effectively.

What you need them to do is create a process vision. You may, for example, have identified resources planning as a central process. Thinking about the key issues affecting this particular process might raise the following issues:

- best possible utilisation of existing resources;
- fair distribution of resources;
- flexibility – resources have to be able to cope with unusual requests;
- peace of mind – people know that promised resources will be delivered;
- access to information – people need to know what the resources available are.

If you need to help a group examining a particular process, a checklist of some of the key ingredients might be useful. Try to work through an individual process from the point of view of each:

Client visit arranged

Send confirmation letter

Client visit

Proposal required?
→ No → Send thank you letter → Copy to marketing for client management system → Filed

Yes → Send thank you letter → Personalised
→ Standard

Check sample proposals

Write proposal

Type proposal

Check proposal

Prepare 6 copies

Bind 5 copies

Inform graphics department for possible presentation material

Prepare covering letter → Personalised
→ Standard

Copy to marketing for client management logging system
Send 3 bound and 1 unbound copy to client with covering letter
→ Fax if urgent
→ Send first class
→ Datapost

Send 1 bound copy to team

Send 1 bound copy to customer information unit

Figure 12.5

- People
- Information
- Finance
- IT
- Goals
- Necessary conditions
- Resources

- Customers
- Owners
- Regulators
- Specialists
- Responsibility
- Skills
- Training

Having worked through these angles you can then more clearly identify issues which concern the people who implement or are affected by the process. By combining their vision of the best possible process, the vision, and the existing tasks which go to make up the process, you can make a start at re-designing a more effective process.

5. RE-DESIGN THE PROCESS

The actual re-design of core processes is where the theory of re-engineering meets the harsh world of corporate reality. Some champions of the re-engineering cause argue that organisations should create a 'clean slate', dispensing with past processes and ways of doing things. They believe that organisations should create a process vision – of a much less pragmatic kind than we suggest – and then implement it. This requires a large investment in terms of money, people, resources and time. Others contend that, in reality, organisations have to accept that there is no clean slate, only a dirty slate which has to be cajoled and moulded into the process vision as far as is humanly possible. The scale of re-design can be divided into four different extremes:

Process tidying – a method by which existing flows of people, information and materials are mapped and streamlined by identifying opportunities for eliminating dead-ends, *ad hoc* activities and duplication.

Process tinkering – a method by which organisations find short-cuts in their processes or identify more user-friendly ways of doing work. In general, process tinkering does not change the overall process nor does it seek to move points of constraints.

Process re-engineering – describes the method by which physical or mental recipe-induced constraints are eliminated from the organisation and re-established in a way which better meets the goals of the organisation.

Process design – this covers the high-level selection of the standard unit process operations to be applied and the selection of appropriate business process configurations (often V, A or T shaped).

6. IMPLEMENTATION PROJECT BY PROJECT

By this stage you should have identified a process vision and have re-designed the process in a way that provides greater efficiency and meets the needs of core constituents. The number of processes you are dealing with depends on the number of blockages, impediments to high performance, which you have identified in the corporate recipe.

You now have to consider how you can turn the visionary process into reality. The skills required to make the change happen are nothing new to managers. They are, in essence, traditional project management skills. Project management is no longer restricted to the engineering world – it is much more than building bridges. Modern methods of project management are now capable of handling changes even when the goals or the means are unclear. Project management can bridge the gap between delivering operational and strategic change. The two types of change are similar, and yet significantly different. Both can be tackled if the process of change is parcelled into deliverable 'chunks' of change rather than being seen in their entirety. However, plenty of questions hang over a project. How do you appraise a five-year re-engineering programme when you are well aware that the goal posts will move during that period? What do you do if, as in re-engineering, a project is interlinked with other projects? How will you handle the increased number of projects and initiatives arising across the organisation in its attempt to re-engineer?

To ensure that re-engineering is implemented project by project, all the links of the project management chain – selection, appraisal and implementation – need to be intact. In re-engineering, companies are taking a step into the unknown, the organisation is extending itself into areas where it has less experience. The risks are made all the more daunting if an organisation fully realises that project failure is equivalent to business failure.

As we have observed earlier, companies which have made the decision to re-engineer often don't know where they want to go. This makes managing far more complex. The projects rely on such non-measurable resources as time, creativity and knowledge. The best chance of success is to work in smaller portions of planning–doing–reviewing.

Few project sponsors will freely admit that they are unsure of what they are doing or how they are going to do it. Instead, they will offer proposals that look concrete. As the project inevitably takes twists and turns which weren't originally anticipated, the initial appraisal is likely to be invalidated fairly quickly. To implement re-engineering project by project requires the following:[9]

Strategic management interpretation – the skills of being able to understand the organisation's strategy and of being capable of contributing to its development in an economic, financial and marketing context. The project leader needs to be able to develop his or her own vision of the change and understand where the organisation's current operations are in conflict with the future needs. This skill ensures that the output the project delivers is in line with the needs of the organisation and that the dilemma of solving tactical and strategic needs is overcome.

Managing a project portfolio – the ability to delegate large portions of the overall project without losing control is a key factor in success. The skills of selecting and monitoring sub-project leaders are highly important. An open project, such as re-engineering, requires an innovator – someone capable of providing business benefits during, as well as at the end of, a changing project.

Invisible leadership – the ability to lead directors, peers and sub-project leaders without becoming ensnared in the political system of the organisation, and of being able to influence without authority and contribute to the overall development of strategy; the skills required to work across different cultures as well as departmental, organisational and often national barriers.

7. PROCESS PITFALLS

As companies grapple with who does what, and where the boundaries between the processes lie, the potential pitfalls are numerous:

- **Avoid identifying too few or too many processes.** If companies go too small they lose a visionary view of the whole business; if they go too big the whole thing become unwieldy and unmanageable, leading to total disruption and confusion. Exxon Chemical International began analysing its processes in the late 1980s. Its vigour was such that processes became highly fragmented and processes which were common across the organisation became confusingly disparate. The result was that regularly undertaken tasks varied greatly even in the same office.

  Rank Xerox claimed at one stage that it had defined 40 or more core processes. Most businesses can be broken into three to five core processes. Rank Xerox now lists seven what it calls 'basic processes'. Any further sub-division means big cross-functional performance improvements may be missed.

- **Do not take the easy route.** A common mistake, inspired by caution as much as anything, is to select what is regarded as an 'easy' process. 'Too often re-engineering addresses non-critical elements of the business,' says David Hall of Boston Consulting Group.[10]
- **Commit time.** Huge investments of senior management's time need to be put into the task of gaining manager's commitment and understanding. If this does not happen then it is unlikely that key processes will be identified or changed.
- **A revolution you can relate to.** It is a waste of time coming up with an intellectually impressive map of the organisation if it is so far away from the existing organisation that managers and staff cannot relate to it. Rank Xerox has made many of its processes appear like functions and uses as much of the former organisation's language and terminology as possible. This may appear to be something of a sell-out – what good is a revolution if it includes vestiges of the old way of doing things? But, in practice, it is a sensible and pragmatic way forward.
- **Integrate, don't isolate.** 'What all but a few companies are doing is really just total quality management – fixing certain processes from the bottom up. So it's not surprising that well-publicised gains in individual processes are failing to be translated into dramatic improvements in the performance of the whole organisation,' says Richard Heygate of consultants McKinsey.[11] Individual processes need to be isolated and analysed. Then, however, they must be put back together into a process-driven structure for the entire organisation.
- **Remember to put a value on change.** It is tempting to select an individual process in a particular business unit, take it to pieces, re-construct it along new lines and then sit back and reap the benefits. Alternatively, managers may fall into the trap of interpreting changes in the process as achievement in itself. They have set themselves a project – to re-engineer a particular process – and success is regarded as the successful re-creation of the process.

If this is to happen, the process must be looked at in broader terms. The cost of the process and its value to customers must be clearly and unequivocally established. Only then can the benefits of change be fully understood and acted upon. It is also worth remembering that re-engineering demands regular injections of radical self-analysis. Re-designed processes can be re-designed at a later stage – often this too can bring significant dividends.

KEY POINTS

1. Identify primary business processes.
2. Remember core constituencies.
3. Make a process visible.
4. Create a process vision.
5. Re-design the process.
6. Implement the re-designed process project by project.

Notes

1 Champy, J & Hammer, M, *Re-engineering the Corporation*, Nicholas Brealey, London, 1993.
2 Harrington, HJ, *Business Process Improvement*, McGraw Hill, Maidenhead, 1991.
3 Devine, M, 'Radical re-engineering', *Directions*, September 1993.
4 Peters, T, 'About turn on integration', *Independent on Sunday*, 5 December 1993.
5 Wheatley, M, 'Boeing Boeing', *Business Life*, December 1993/January 1994.
6 Dickson, T, 'A source of best practice', *Financial Times*, 20 August 1993.
7 Pudney, R, 'The power of partnerships', *Directions*, September 1993.
8 Hall, G, Rosenthal, J & Wade, J, 'How to make re-engineering really work', *Harvard Business Review*, November–December 1993.
9 Obeng, EDA, *All Change!*, FT/Pitman, London, 1994.
10 Lorenz, C, 'Sculptors in jelly', *Financial Times*, 28 July 1993.
11 Lorenz, C, 'Sculptors in jelly', *Financial Times*, 28 July 1993.

3

MAKING THE MOST OF INFORMATION

INFORMATION AS A SUPPORT

Information underpins the re-engineered organisation. Not information in the primary process, but rather information in the secondary process. The example used previously on the process behind a proposal has been reproduced diagramatically in order to highlight the points at which information (in this case usually computer-based) serves the process (see Figure 13.1). The process itself is written in a format within which each process step contains a verb and an object but no subject. The subject, as we will describe later, is the resource to which the task falls, while the object will form the basis of any object-orientation required in the supporting database.

Information or data are supplied or retrieved into the primary process by the supporting information infrastructure. By splitting the process in this fashion it is possible to introduce a process with a supportive relational database which provides the flexibility required of a re-engineered process. An over-riding influence of information in a re-engineered organisation is its overall pervasiveness. Proportionately, more effort should be put into identifying process information needs than into the design of the process itself because it is only by establishing the information needs that a process, which captures the appropriate data, can be designed.

Information also requires forethought in terms of storage and manipulation of data and its transfer. This depends on the type of information sought. In *The Virtual Corporation*, Davidow and Malone identify various types of information. These are: 'form information' (this is concerned with how an object is made up and deals, often at length, on specifications); 'behaviour information' (such as using IT to simulate a product's behaviour in a particular environment); and 'action information' (the conversion of the information into action).

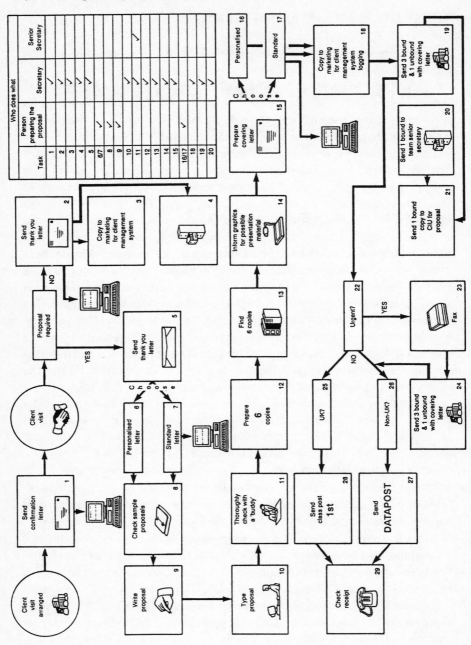

Figure 13.1 A business process map

RESOURCE MIS-MANAGEMENT

Resource management is closely intertwined with re-engineering's approach to processes and people. The re-engineered organisation has to learn anew how to assign its non-human resources to the needs of processes and enable people to fulfil their tasks more efficiently. As with other aspects of re-engineering, managers are liable to throw their hands in the air and say, 'We do that already, our resource management is second to none'. This is rarely the case. How many times have you had to explain to a customer that you haven't been able to do something because you are waiting for another department to deliver? How many times have you received reams of data from another department and have then had to wade through thousands of statistics before you reach the one piece of information you really need, and asked for? How many times have you cursed the marketing department's concentration of its resources to back a particular product?

Our experience suggests that these sorts of problems are commonplace in most organisations. Resources are rarely applied systematically, in a measurable way, or to the places which most need them. Re-engineering demands that organisations return to first principles and establish what resources they possess, how they are organised and how they are utilised.

Any single process relies on a regular supply of resources, whether these are the specific skills of individuals, information or materials. Take the process we highlighted earlier, covering the tasks involved in generating a proposal. Here we place the resources required next to the task:

1. Client visit arranged: account manager
2. Send confirmation letter: secretary
3. Client visit: account team
4. Send thank you letter: account manager, secretary
5. Copy to marketing for client management system: person responsible for marketing database
6. Check sample proposals: account manager; person responsible for holding past proposals
7. Write proposal: account manager
8. Type proposal: secretary
9. Check proposal: account manager and colleague
10. Prepare 6 copies: secretary
11. Bind 5 copies: secretary
12. Inform graphics department for possible presentation material: account manager; graphics department

13. Prepare covering letter: account manager; secretary
14. Copy to marketing for client management logging system: person responsible for marketing database
15. Send copies to client: secretary
16. Distribute copy to account team: secretary; account manager
17. Send copy to customer information unit: person in charge of customer information

This is a relatively simple process, yet it involves a number of people from throughout the organisation. Within each of these stages the people require a supply of other resources – for example, stationery, telephones, etc. Many informal links are also likely to be established. The account manager will, for example, want to find out more about the prospective client's business. He or she will make a variety of contacts to find out this information. As the process unfolds they will also be keeping other managers up to date with progress and keeping in touch with individual departments who will deliver the final product.

There are no surprises in this process. Such activities are happening every day of the week. But, consider some of the impediments to this occurring:

- The information provided on the prospective customer is out of date and causes the account manager severe embarrassment when the wrong figures are quoted.
- There is no central system to manage previous proposals – the account manager has to invent the proposal from scratch.
- The graphics department says it hasn't got the time to prepare slides on the off-chance the organisation gets the new business.
- The secretary is now working for two people and sends the proposal out later than promised to the client.
- The chief executive insists on showing the clients around and mentions a service you no longer provide.
- The marketing department fails to inform the account manager that his or her predecessor tried unsuccessfully to sell the same service to the prospective clients.

Most of these failures can be attributed to a greater or lesser extent to resources. While it is unlikely that any one process is going to encounter all of them, a single event can knock the entire process off the rails.

These sorts of problems are symptomatic of the way functional organisations utilise their resources. Instead of being driven by organisational goals, resources are often driven by functional prejudices and objectives. Indeed, in many cases, resources have become buried within individual functions to the extent that it is difficult to extract them when they are desperately needed. In the functional organisation resources are often jealously guarded. Individual functions dispense their resources to colleagues with caution. The re-engineered organisation, however, regards resources as a vital lubricant to its activities, a means of getting things done quicker and more efficiently.

THE RE-INVENTION OF MARKETING

Organisations where resources *are* provided in a timely and supportive way are not pie in the sky – already many organisations are questioning how to make use of some of their previously untouchable resources. As an example, look at the changing fortunes and perception of the marketing resource.

Clearly, marketing is a core activity of any organisation. Its role is often critical to success. Marketing identifies customer needs, suggests products to satisfy the demand and then operates a follow-up support system to ensure consumer satisfaction. The marketing department is the mouthpiece of the customer in the organisation. The 1980s saw the apotheosis of marketing. Its importance was more widely recognised than ever before. Companies championed themselves as being market-driven. Budgets swelled and senior marketing managers were given a place on the board of many organisations. At the beginning of the 1990s there was a shift in attitudes and practice. Some organisations have realised that, despite their talk of being market-driven and market-focused, they have instead become *marketing*-driven and *marketing*-focused. Marketing is not any less important but, instead of dispensing blank cheques to marketing departments, companies are beginning to question and examine the role and achievement of marketing managers in attaining their objectives. No resource is an island and organisations want to establish how marketing best fits and relates to the rest of the organisation and, most importantly, how effective it is in meeting the needs of customers. There is no point in having a corporate lubricant if all it does is support cyclical motion in a narrowly defined area.

Financial services company Allied Dunbar is an archetypal example of an organisation which flourished in the 1980s, thanks to effective marketing, and lost its way in the early 1990s. In 1991, a new chief executive began a radical process of assessment. It was discovered that the company had a distorted view of its marketplace, relying on a 'market segmentation' model which had little connection with the changing demographics of reality.

Allied Dunbar set about finding out what clients thought of the company and what they expected from it. As a result, it hopes to be able to measure the relationship between client satisfaction and profitability – this will enable marketing to be properly directed and be more responsive to customer needs.

Other organisations have come to similar realisations. The malaise now identified in the marketing operation of many organisations is a functional one. Often, marketing departments have not only failed to build close relationships with customers, but have isolated themselves within their own organisations. A 1993 survey of 100 UK companies by management consultants Coopers & Lybrand found huge disparities between what marketing departments think they contribute and what everyone else feels.[1] A third of marketing directors think they are entirely or mainly responsible for strategic planning; but only one-fifth of managing directors agree.

The Coopers & Lybrand report also demonstrated that most procedures for measuring the effectiveness of marketing activity are irrelevant and result in a lack of accountability. A total of 57 per cent of companies used sales revenue to measure effectiveness; 53 per cent used market share; 39 per cent used net profit to measure marketing effectiveness. It concluded that the effective marketing department of the future will:

- have within its remit all the processes that contribute to managing the customer and consumer interface;
- have clear and defined responsibility for these processes;
- focus on activities that demonstrably add value;
- be measured, and judged against these measures.[2]

Some companies are already re-organising their marketing resources so that they become more truly aligned to the needs of customers, interact more effectively with the rest of the organisation, and are treated as a process rather than as an unwieldy and often isolated department. Marketing needs to re-define and re-engineer its role and organisation for the future. In *Tomorrow's Competition*, Mack Hanan, sums up this challenge. The modern marketing challenge, writes Hanan, is to 'make your business competitive by making the businesses of your customers more competitive.'[3]

One company tackling the issue is Elida Gibbs, the UK personal products subsidiary of Unilever. Its brands include Fabergé Brut, Pears, Signal and Timotei. In a revolutionary move, Elida Gibbs abolished the post of brand manager and re-invented the sales team as the 'customer development process'. Brands are now the responsibility of brand development managers.

The changes at Elida Gibbs stem from criticisms of its performance in the late 1980s. Poor delivery standards and an old-fashioned ordering system were a source of irritation to customers. As a result, Elida Gibbs introduced teamworking at one of its factories in 1988. Responsibility for each production line was transferred to those working on it. As well as these changes, Elida Gibbs reduced the number of its suppliers and gave suppliers more responsibility for quality control, testing and development. The roles of the company's managers were also re-defined on the basis of processes. Functional divisions were replaced by 'seamless teams'. Many of the day-to-day contacts with retailers, which used up brand managers' time, have been passed on to customer development managers. Over the last three years change-over time on one production line has been reduced to less than four hours, when it previously took an entire day. In addition, 90 per cent of orders are now correctly completed – against 72 per cent in the past. Between 1989 and 1991 the company's pre-tax profits rose by 73 per cent and margins widened from 6.5 per cent to 10 per cent. In April 1993 Elida Gibbs launched its first major product since its internal changes. It involved a development process of less than six months – half as much time as development had previously taken.

Similarly, SmithKline Beecham has spent much of 1993 overhauling its marketing activities. It believed it had been hampered by the company being divided into geographic units. SmithKline Beecham studied other companies, including Procter and Gamble and Unilever, and then set up six teams – each responsible for a product category. The teams were given free rein to co-opt managers from national subsidiaries. Sales in consumer brands rose by 11 per cent in 1993 and product development cycles have been accelerated – a new toothbrush was developed in 40 per cent of the previous time.[4]

Harvard Business School's Benson Shapiro argues that truly market-driven companies have three characteristics:

- Information on all important buying influences permeates every corporate function.
- Strategic and tactical decisions are made inter-functionally and inter-divisionally.
- Divisions and functions make well-co-ordinated decisions and execute them with a sense of commitment.[5]

Re-engineering seeks to address all of these issues. The use of cross-functional teams and the dismantling of functional divides allows crucial market information to circulate more easily and more widely throughout the organisation. Teamworking leads to more decisions being made by people working through the issues and available information together. Finally, clear understanding of the organisational goals and core constituencies leads to marketing decisions being made within an overall process of measurable performance rather than as isolated one-offs.

The rigorous process of analysis to which many organisations are subjecting their marketing operations, should form an integral part of any re-engineering programme. While we have highlighted the marketing fucntion, many, if not all, of the lessons are applicable to other parts of the organisation. Within all traditional functions, instead of being internalised, isolated and thought of in functional terms, resources need to be unlocked.

USING THE IT RESOURCE

The corporate resource which has, perhaps, the largest role to play in re-engineering is IT. The world IT market is expected to reach a massive $700 billion by 1997 – yet, as we have seen, IT has so far failed to yield the productivity and performance benefits anticipated by managers and organisations. The reasons for this are many and varied. One central reason is that managers often have only a limited understanding of what IT can do for their organisation. They have a broad sympathy with investing in high technology, but have a restricted view of its practical power and business advantage. For example, a survey by Henley Management College of more than 200 chief executives, directors and other senior managers found that many top managers just did not understand the strategic importance of IT.

We believe that a great many managers, if asked, would identify the benefits of IT in simple cost terms. IT reduces an organisation's staff count, therefore it saves money. As Shoshana Zuboff points out in her book, *In the Age of the Smart Machine*, companies have regarded IT as a means of reducing staff numbers through the automation of their jobs. The trouble is that the jobs which have been automated out of existence are often those which involve direct contact with customers. Zuboff argues that instead of automating tasks, IT's job should be to 'informate' people – an ungainly, but apposite, word combining inform and educate. By regarding IT as a numbers and cost-cutting mechanism organisations are failing to optimise its full potential which goes far beyond cost reduction.

While managers are comfortable with the concept of cost control and reduction, they find it difficult to come to terms with other implications of IT. With limited knowledge managers find that they are unable to bring the same reporting and measuring disciplines to bear when some new IT product is introduced. A large investment in a new machine on the production line inevitably means that every effort is made by the company to measure and monitor the performance and productivity increases which the machine brings. The machine's *raison d'être* is simple and well understood. If, however, managers invest in a costly new IT system, not only is it likely that they cannot use it – even though it could help them in their work – but they have no idea how, and often little inclination, to measure its productivity benefits accurately. They may calculate direct cost savings but, in many cases, the more widespread advantages are assumed, with productivity gains neither monitored nor measured. A UK survey carried out by Computervision Services, a support services company, shows that nine out of ten managers believe office networks contribute significantly to productivity – but only one in ten measures the gains. Organisations expect an average increase of 65 per cent in the number of office network users during 1994, but 40 per cent of companies and 80 per cent of public sector bodies do not make any business case for network purchases.[6]

When it comes to IT, managers appear to suspend their disbelief and allow IT experts to get on with it. Managers also tend to have limited expertise in managing the obsessive enthusiasts who hone in on computer departments. It is not, perhaps, surprising that managers struggle to come to terms with IT – IT often unsettles their ways of working. IT may provide managers with information they have previously been starved of and sometimes never knew existed. Suddenly there is a deluge of statistical data and making a decision becomes ever more complex. As a result, there is the strong temptation to nod knowingly when the data falls on to your desk and carry on using the parameters and measurements you have always used as the basis for your decision-making. Managers remain fearful of falling into the trap described by Gertrude Stein: 'Everybody gets so much information all day long that they lose their commonsense'.

Using IT for the wrong jobs

A second factor in the failure of IT to boost productivity as significantly as it should, is the fact that it is often used for the wrong jobs. Quality programmes, for example, have often exacerbated this situation to the extent that IT becomes marginalised. Instead of being regarded as a core tool by which quality and improved productivity can be achieved, IT has been treated simply as a means of collecting data and ensuring that quality processes are backed by sound statistics.

Part of the problem is that IT is sometimes regarded as a data-gathering device and little else. Unquestionably, IT is the best possible tool for organisations to gather a huge range of data about their business and its performance. The crunch comes when data is turned into information – this requires that companies have the systems, processes and people in place to ask the right questions to convert data to information. Data remains data until you ask a question. Information is the answer to the question.

While IT has been used as a means of data-gathering, the emphasis of its practical use has also been on managing the links between different divisions, functions and activities rather than with customers. IT has traditionally looked at what departments do and then provided them with information. It has made an organisation's internal life and system easier to handle rather than providing improved service to customers.

Often IT is backed by an individual department or function which identifies ways by which IT can make its work more efficient. These do not, however, necessarily apply across the entire organisation. The end-result is that a number of different systems emerge with little in the way of linkages between them or overall strategy. 'Companies must remain flexible in their IT strategy. Those that declare that open systems are the only way forward may be left in the wake of the Windows rush. Technicians are fond of declaring which is the best operating system but that often has little to do with its success or failure in the market,' says Kevin Grumball, of computer consultants Software Design & Construction. 'It is essential that any IT strategy embraces all the aims of the company rather than taking a parochial view.'[7]

The conventional approach to IT fails to see it in broader strategic terms. IT is regarded as a means of doing existing jobs faster. The obvious corollary of this is that organisations often make the same mistakes at twice the speed.

IT's role in re-engineering

An article in the *California Management Review* describes the organisation of the future as one which is 'dynamically stable', 'capable of serving the widest range of customers and changing product demands (dynamic) while building on long-term process capabilities and the collective knowledge of the organisation (stable)'. IT is identified as the crucial weapon in achieving this paradoxical combination.[8]

Q

- How does IT link your organisation to customers?
- How do you measure the productivity gains brought by IT?
- Is IT managed and controlled by a single function?
- Has IT provided you with data or information?
- How has IT helped you provide customers with better service?

In re-engineering, IT takes a central role as a key **enabler** of entirely new, cross-functional business processes. An example is in the use of relational databases which enable workers to relate data on what is happening in sales, marketing, operations and finance. This brings functional, horizontal and vertical integration and asks fundamental questions as to what is the nature of the task to be performed and by whom. IT overcomes functional divides. Even so, many organisations still segment data on a functional basis, reflecting industrial organisational design, and fail to exploit the relational nature of technology, acquired in the 1980s and now technologically mature. They forget that advances in technology mean that information can appear simultaneously in many places as it is needed – not just in one place at one time.

This ability to put information simultaneously in the hands of those who need to know – regardless of function or location – enables organisations to break the sequential nature of functional processes for radical improvements in productivity. 'In most cases, the greatest practical strategic leverage of IT lies not in some IT-driven company overhaul from top-to-bottom, but in the ability of IT to support the re-design of a company's working practices – that is, its established routines, procedures, techniques and approaches for accomplishing core tasks and activities – as well as its organisational structures,' say Richard Heygate and Greg Brebach of management consultants McKinsey.[9]

Clearly, IT is one of the key tools of re-engineering. Indeed, it should be one of the key tools of any business which genuinely wishes to move closer to its customers. Many organisations have already succeeded in using IT to provide imaginative solutions and create opportunities:

Responsiveness. Frank's Nursery and Crafts in Detroit can supply additional stock to its stores when the weekend weather forecast is good. It uses IT to anticipate demand.

US retailer Wal-Mart approached Procter and Gamble, pointing out that it should remind Wal-Mart when to re-order as P&G knows its business and customers better. As a result, P&G manages and finances the Pampers inventory thanks to direct links between Wall-Mart's check-out system and P&G's ordering system.

Customers of the Dutch PTT can sort out the installation of a new telephone with a single visit to one of the company's offices. This includes a contract, a new number and the time of connection – now made within two days as opposed to the previous two weeks. By 1995 connections will be made on the spot. Dutch PTT achieved this level of responsiveness by taking the information from its huge mainframe computers and channelling them to individual terminals in sales offices. Instead of switching from one system to another to find all the relevant information – such as on debtors – operators can now locate it easily and quickly.

The IT system used by the Florida-based Home Shopping Network is such that its data is updated every ten seconds. This means that the presenters on TV who are selling the products can see how well each is doing. If the charming ceramic rhino is selling badly they can move on to the truly amazing electronic gadget. With this system, HSN can calculate its performance in 'dollars per minute'.

Q

- Have your organisation's senior managers received IT training?

- Who makes IT buying decisions?

- Who has a say from outside the IT department?

- Does IT make you more effective?

- What performance does your organisation measure through IT?

- Are you provided with data or information?

- Who measures the performance effectiveness of your IT systems?

Flexibility. Home Shopping Network answers customer orders with a recorded voice called 'Tootie'. The computerised system will take people's order, sort out how they are going to pay and instruct the warehouse to despatch the product to their home address. Not all customers like the idea of speaking to a computer, even one called Tootie. But, if the customer does not speak to Tootie within five seconds, her dulcet tones are immediately replaced by a live operator.

Improving performance. The US's Federal National Mortgage Association (Fannie Mae) found that its huge computer system simply could not cope with the growth of its business. In response, it broke down time-consuming departmental divides and installed a network of 2,000 PCs with new easy-to-use software. Costing $10 million, it was a sizeable investment – it paid for itself in less than a year. Though volume doubled between 1991 and 1993, the company took on a mere 100 extra people to cope with the soaring demand. In 1993 Fannie Mae's profits reached $1.87 billion thanks to the company serving a record 3.3 million families through mortgage purchases and security guarantees.

Working with customers. 'We know exactly where we want to go, because our customers will show us the way. Our customers know the solutions they need. It's our job to bring them solutions, through the application of technology,' says Jerre Stead, chief executive of AT&T Global Information Solutions.[10] IT bridges gaps between organisations and their customers. DuPont no longer expects invoices from some of its vendors. Instead, it just processes bills electronically. With about five per cent of its suppliers the company doesn't even bother with purchase orders. Outside suppliers are linked electronically with DuPont's internal inventory system. When suppliers see DuPont is running short on an item they deliver replacement goods.

'Most large organisations are now seeing IT as one of the most important bridges to enhancing customer service. They now rarely see customer service as having separate components, such as marketing, selling, after-sales service and invoicing, each with their own system,' says Merlin Stone, visiting professor at Kingston University and a partner in Avanti Consultancy services.[11]

Bringing people closer together. Expert systems enable non-specialists to carry out what were once specialised tasks. IT should be a means of bringing people closer together and breaking down barriers.

NEXT STEPS

1. THINKING RESOURCES NOT FUNCTIONS

Interactive marketing enables marketing miracles to become commonplace. You can call a number and the company will instantly be able to take advantage of a large amount of information about you. Organisations can develop interactive relationships with their customers. Is this a triumph for marketing or IT? Who should take responsibility for a database of an individual customer's transactions with your organisation? The answer is that it is everyone's responsibility. Organisations now need to think of functions in terms of resources. Examine the resources controlled and utilised by a particular function in your organisations:

- What specialist knowledge does the function possess?
- How accessible is that knowledge to others in the organisation?
- What non-human resources does the function control?
- If you want to use a particular function's resources how do you go about doing it?
- What resources do you control?
- How do other parts of the organisation use these resources?

It is only by seeing and using functions as resources that re-engineering can work. Part of the problem with the way IT has been utilised is that it has become yet another function when it should be a prime resource. Organisations are now, as a result, having to re-engineer their IT function – according to research in the US, organisations are set to invest a massive $40 billion in re-engineering their information systems in 1997. Acerbically, William Wheeler of Coopers & Lybrand, told *Fortune magazine*: 'That's putting whipped cream on garbage.'[12]

The managing director of a logistics services company told us he was very proud of the fact that instead of buying more vehicles he invested in computers. The vehicles would deliver things to customers, but the computers, he believed, 'will invade the processes of my customers'. We believe that the key impediment in many organisations to the full utilisation of IT lies among senior managers. This can only be tackled through a process of continuous education and development. Managers have to learn to appreciate new IT skills – they don't have to know exactly what various applications involve, but they do need to have some idea of the potential use.

2. IDENTIFY THE ROLE OF IT

For IT to play a full role in enabling re-engineering to happen, it has to be involved in the process from the very beginning. The temptation in many organisations is for groups of managers to generate exciting re-designed processes and then turn to the IT specialist and ask what they can provide to fit the particular specification. In doing so, many of the potential benefits and applications of IT can be overlooked. If the IT department is involved from the very outset their input can ensure that opportunities are taken rather than overlooked. Only by considering IT capabilities and overall organisational goals at the same time are major advances likely to be made.

IT's role in enabling re-engineering to happen can take on a variety of forms. These may include:

- reducing human resources required to fulfil a particular task or process;
- process analysis – IT can prove extremely helpful as organisations struggle to capture accurately their own processes;
- decision making – IT can improve analysis and provide new decision-making capabilities for individual managers who have more information, and groups or teams who can make decisions together using IT as a tool;
- improving processes – not only is IT capable of reducing the number of people involved in the process, but it can allow them to be managed successfully from a different or distant location, thereby ridding the process of intermediary tasks.

To convert IT from a blockage to an enabler requires that the organisation clearly identifies the business benefits of IT. These can include: faster and more accurate communication of information; elimination of certain manual tasks; more informed decision-making; potential for increased teamworking; and delegation of responsibility. The company then has to identify its organisational needs. First, what information does it need to perform as efficiently as possible? Remember the process we looked at earlier, involving the various tasks involved in selecting, buying, planting and maintaining plants.

Each task in this process requires a certain amount of information. Take the task of going to the nursery. The necessary information to perform this efficiently may include: the nearest nursery; the cheapest; the expert on plants, etc. All the other tasks require similar amounts of information and for the purchaser to make decisions based on this information. Many of the tasks involved in a particular process require a great amount of information.

IT's role, therefore, is to provide the right kind of information to the right people at the right time in the process.

● PREPARE SEED BED	● PLANT PLANTS
● CHECK BUDGET	● GO TO NURSERY
● DIG THEM UP AGAIN	● WEED AND LOOK AFTER
● CHOOSE STYLE OF BED	PLANTS
	● CHOOSE PLANTS

Key Technologies

● **Graphical user interfaces** – these devices make computers far easier to use than ever before. Graphics on the screen have the characteristics of the real thing.

● **Networking software** – networked managers and workers can work together despite geographical separation. Timetables, diaries, memos and reports can be constantly and easily communicated.

● **Flexible databases** – relational databases share and transmit information throughout the organisation and can be as responsive to include changes every time a transaction is made.

● **Imaging** – this software enables people in the same organisation to read the same document simultaneously. In an insurance company, for example, the same claim may be examined by two separate people on screen at the same time rather than being passed from one to the other.

Notes

1 Coopers & Lybrand, *Marketing at the Crossroads*, Coopers & Lybrand, London, 1993.
2 Coopers & Lybrand, *Marketing at the Crossroads*, Coopers & Lybrand, London, 1993.
3 Hanan, M, *Tomorrow's Competition*, AMACOM, New York, 1991.
4 Jonquieres, G de, 'Buying the Bactroban with the bath oil', *Financial Times*, 10 January 1994.
5 Shapiro, B, 'What the hell is market oriented?', *Harvard Business Review*, November–December 1988.
6 Kavanagh, J, 'The fun starts when users switch on', *Financial Times Software at Work*, Winter 1993.

7 Grumball, K, 'Consultant's Critique', *Financial Times*, 14 December 1993.
8 Boynton, A, 'Achieving dynamic stability through IT', *California Management Review*, Vol. 35, No. 2, Winter 1993.
9 Heygate, R & Brebach, G, 'Rethinking the corporation', *McKinsey Quarterly*, No. 2, 1991.
10 Advertisement in *Financial Times*, 27 January 1994.
11 Fisher, A, 'Speed is of the essence', *Financial Times*, 3 August 1993.
12 Carr, D, et al., *Breakpoint*, Coopers & Lybrand, Arlington, Virginia, 1992.

4

GETTING PEOPLE ON BOARD

THE HARD SIDE OF SOFT ISSUES

Most of the extensive theorising and practice in the field of re-engineering pays scant attention to the concerns and fears of the people involved in making it happen. Talk of turbulence and the relentless progress of change through global business is easy. Talk of the effects of upheaval and change on individual managers and employees is less straightforward, fraught as it is with fears and disappointment. The challenge was described by Niccolo Machiavelli:

> It should be borne in mind that there is nothing more difficult to arrange, more doubtful of success and more dangerous to carry through than initiating changes in a state's constitution. The innovator makes enemies of all those who prospered under the old order and only lukewarm support is forthcoming from those who would prosper under the new.

Re-engineering involves more than analysing processes and re-structuring organisations. 'There are many examples of so-called business process re-engineering that, at the end of the day, find the changing of culture and people too difficult. Hence, only processes and systems are changed. It is much easier to re-design procedures and throw in some technology, than to embark upon the long uphill struggle of changing people's attitudes, beliefs and values,' says consultant Chris Skinner.[1] Change, if it is to work, must involve and alter the perceptions and behaviour of people.

The lengthy catalogue of failed change and quality programmes is testament to the general neglect of the people side of such initiatives and, when it is identified, of the failure of organisations to come to terms with it. A survey by KPMG Management Consulting of top executives in 250 UK companies found that only 31 per cent believed that their change programmes were 'very effective'.[2] 'Identifying the need for change is relatively straightforward, what really causes problems is making change happen successfully,' the KPMG survey reports.

To be effective, change has to carry people along with it. The 'lukewarm support' described by Machiavelli will stop any change programme in its tracks. A programme which looks good in the boardroom can remain a theoretical ideal if people do not commit themselves to the change process. Re-engineering is no different. Indeed, the changes it intends to bring about are far beyond those usually contemplated in total quality programmes or the like.

The early concentration of re-engineering programmes has been on tackling the 'hard' issues – such as processes and systems. Indeed, re-engineering is often preceded by the words 'business process' to suggest that processes are the beginning and end of the programme. They are, however, only part of the battle. The 'soft' issues – people, skills, behaviour, culture and values – are at least as critical, often more so. They, too, have a hard side.

The people-related issues are here to stay. In 1992–93 the US economy grew by 2.6 per cent, but over 500,000 clerical and technical positions disappeared, probably for good.[3] A survey by *3i* in the UK found that early in 1994 – after the worst of recession was supposedly over – two-thirds of companies expected a further reduction in middle management numbers.[4] Dealing with the ramifications of such a massive displacement of people is fundamental to the success or failure of any change or re-engineering programme. Not only do managers often have to deal sympathetically with redundancies, but they also have to convince those who remain in the organisation of the logic for, and the necessity of, the change.

DOES CULTURE CHANGE COME FIRST?

There is an on-going debate over whether behavioural and cultural change – through empowerment, teamworking, etc. – is an inherent result of re-engineering, or whether it needs to be launched before re-engineering begins. In the US, for example, Bell Atlantic set up its culture change programme two years before beginning the re-engineering process. At the centre of this discussion is the common belief that a changed organisational structure, or more radical re-organisation, naturally leads to a change in corporate culture. Though this may be the case, changing organisational cultures is a lengthy, time-consuming and delicate process. Re-engineering does, by its very nature, involve cultural change. It emphasises how organisations *are* as well as what they *do*.

US insurance company, Cigna, has learned – through experience – that cultural change needs to precede re-engineering, if only by a few months. Its initial efforts were hampered by the fact that it had not held preparatory meetings involving all staff. When the changes came, staff were, as a result, poorly prepared to accept radical changes in corporate thinking and its entire language. In the middle of 1991 Cigna's UK operation, Cigna Employee Benefits, which specialises in group health insurance, began the process of changing its culture before the full-blown re-engineering programme began. Regular meetings explained what re-engineering and teamwork involved, and what would be expected of people in the new environment. When cross-departmental processes and teamworking were put in place, the meetings continued as a way of reviewing and monitoring achievements and to set goals.

Cigna's UK operations have, through re-engineering, transformed six separate business functions into two processes. The processes are based around pre- and post-sales activities. As a result, the time it takes to give a quote has been cut from 17 days to two, and staff who used to process between 35 and 40 claims a day can now handle 75 to 90. These changes, coupled with a move to a new location, have slashed over 1 million from the company's costs. The unit's underwriting loss of 2 million in 1992 has been turned into profitability.

The key to Cigna's approach is talking to managers and staff to see what they think, and fear, about change. Instead of ignoring or firing those who oppose re-engineering, Cigna has taken a more assertive route by appointing them to key positions of responsibility. Only five per cent of staff have left the company.

Managers are put in an unusual position – one many would find difficult to cope with. While some aspects of their jobs are taken over by junior employees, they are entrusted with the responsibility of changing the organisation into a radical new shape and culture. Cigna's approach is to get on with re-engineering rather than theorising or spending weeks analysing processes. It brought people from administration, claims and accounts and simply moved them around a single desk. Managers carried on as normal and the group's productivity increased. This sort of flexibility allows the cross-functional teams to design their own process rather than working to the dictate of someone else's creation. Susan Kozik, Cigna vice-president observes: 'After our first programmes we learnt that you can trust the teams. Management who tried to hand down changes were missing out on the most knowledgeable group of people. For smaller process changes we now allow staff to design the new processes. For broader changes we use the teams as a source of ideas.' Putting such faith in teams made up of relatively junior employees does not come easily – in the US some of the Cigna divisions have been tentative about starting the programme in such a way.

Cigna's approach of allowing teams to develop their own processes has one obvious advantage – having created the process themselves the team is more likely to feel a sense of ownership. In effect, the creation of the process works as an important means of cultural change. 'You cannot clone re-engineering. This is not something you can learn from a book. It's about people and personalities,' says Susan Kozik.[5]

It is unlikely that successful cultural change can be made in a wholesale way. The past is not easily dismissed – nor should you want to dispense totally with some of the more positive and established ways of thinking and working. Marrying the old and new cultures is a formidable balancing act.

Engineering company, Whessoe, had, over its 200 years existence, formed a formidable reputation for quality engineering. As its business developed so did the basic premise – its recipe – that the highest possible quality was the core of the business; everything else would then fall into place. Under a new management team the company has, since 1990, begun the process of re-inventing itself and its culture. It withdrew from its traditional business and moved into instrumentation. It also dispensed with age-old demarcation. Now, shopfloor workers have the same terms and conditions as the rest of the staff – the result has been an end to demarcation disputes. The trouble faced by Whessoe, and many others businesses in traditional industries, is that in re-creating itself in a new market it runs the risk of distancing itself from its past achievements and reputation.

Whessoe has managed to combine continuity with radical change. 'One of the dangers . . . is that you can lose a lot of the knowledge acquired by the business over many years,' says chief executive Chris Fleetwood. The board now includes two directors steeped in experience of the old culture. 'Management in industry tends to underestimate what is possible. We tend to look for incremental improvements of five or ten per cent. But in instrumentation it is possible to make those quantum leaps of 200 per cent and that, I feel, is where our future should be,' says Fleetwood.[6]

One organisation which has firmly set out to change its culture first is the UK's eighth largest building society, National and Provincial (N&P). Its emphasis is on changing the overall culture of the organisation and creating a new organisational structure. Unlike many others, it has started the process at the top with an emphasis on 'process leadership'. N&P aims to get managers committed and then actively change the way they operate rather than working from the bottom up. So far, the majority of N&P's 4,000 strong workforce remain untouched by the process.

N&P's programme was instigated by a new management team of David O'Brien and Paul Chapman, who took over in 1990. Their first step was to arrange a week of meetings with the heads of the company's businesses and senior corporate personnel – a small group of around ten people. A new mission statement was then produced based around customer requirements. The board was re-named the 'direction management team' and its operations were divided into a 'direction management process'. Functional and business leaders were re-incarnated as directors of 'customer engagement' and 'customer requirements'. To further the process, during 1991, 150 of the company's senior managers were addressed in small groups and the planned changes explained to them. Only 25 left the company.

From a structural point of view, N&P's intention is to reduce its eight levels of management and more than 20 grades to three levels and four grades. The process is now being supported by a system of competency assessment and performance-related pay. The skills required for particular jobs or roles are analysed so that the right person is fitted to the right job. This relies heavily on self-assessment and discussion at branch level. As yet, N&P has not moved on to the next stage of its re-engineering programme – the introduction of a new IT system which will cost around £20 million.

N&P's approach has much to recommend. By concentrating on management processes the organisation relays a clear message that management is no longer untouchable. If employees have seen managers being put through a process of re-education and re-definition, and have seen the operational benefits, they are more likely to support changes in their own working practices.

An important element in this cultural change can be seen in N&P's introduction of new job titles. Re-engineering brings with it a new language for organisations. Indeed, changing job titles is a very useful tool in encouraging people to begin to look at their jobs in a different light.

HOW DO PEOPLE VIEW CHANGE?

Despite the pervasiveness of ideas about how re-engineering can work, they have not yet penetrated the assumptions of most managers. In fact, the entire concept of change is not readily accepted. Change is often the last resort. Companies which have gained the most from re-engineering tend to be those that have been required to change through market pressure, plummeting profitability, or even the prospect of imminent bankruptcy. In such circumstances, the directors are prepared to take drastic steps to turn the company around. The trouble is that many more companies need to re-engineer to prevent themselves reaching this situation.

As a starting point it is worth considering how you view change. Try drawing a picture representing your conception of change. On training programmes we have asked managers to do the same exercise. It is striking how often these depict a relatively static model. Commonly this involves moving from a stable position, via a short period of uncertainty, to a new and different, but again relatively stable position. Managers continue to regard successful change as establishing a new order, structure or *status quo*. In their eyes, the process involves stepping from one position to a new one within a discrete time.

'We've been through massive changes on the shop floor in the last 12 months,' observed the production manager of a large engineering company. 'We now need five to six years to bed down the new systems and methods of working.' In reality, a year later the production unit had been closed down as part of the company's rationalisation. The management thought the unit was unable to change sufficiently to meet increasing competitive pressures. The dedication to 'bedding down' change, led to corporate coma. There is no rest from the process of change.

HOW MANAGERS SEE CHANGE

- Logical
- Short-term
- Linear
- Sequential
- Incremental
- Requires slight alterations in the way they work
- Manageable
- Able to be halted if there are problems

In another example, a multinational which had been successfully keeping abreast, if not ahead, of its markets, carried out a staff attitude survey which showed staff felt that the pace of change was excessive, perhaps unnecessary. Many favoured a period of stability. Similarly, a newly appointed European product manager assured us that, having changed from a structure based in national subsidiaries to a pan-European structure, several years were needed to 'let it settle down'.

At another company a staff meeting allowed people to express their disquiet about what they considered was a period of excessive instability, where new staff had been brought in at a rapid rate and the entire structure of the company shaken up. The chief executive stood up, his audience expecting a placatory statement, to announce that they hadn't seen anything yet – change was there to stay and would become even more fast moving in the future. The message was simple – stay and adapt or leave.

The key difference between re-engineering and other change programmes is that in re-engineering change often appears to be illogical. By its very nature, proactive change is harder to rationalise and communicate than reactive change where you can point to specific events which have already occurred and are having a clear effect on the business. Indeed, initial responses are emotional – anger, fear, insecurity – though, over time, they may become accepted as logical.

Incremental change .... Response: logical
Re-engineering .... Response: emotional

For managers this represents an immense challenge. In the past, if a person was made redundant managers could usually explain the decision clinically and rationally. They could, more often than not, attribute blame to external factors such as depressed demand. With re-engineering the argument is less easy for managers to put forward – they are saying that they are making changes for the future, or simply that the person's work does not add value to what the company does. Similar difficulties arise in explaining decisions to the people who remain.

HOW PEOPLE REACT TO RE-ENGINEERING

Having analysed processes and removed repetitive or needless activities, organisations have a clear view of the processes necessary to satisfy their core stakeholders. But, by its very definition, this requires flexible and variable inputs from people. Employees lose the security of job specialisms and set procedures, while managers suddenly find their performance under closer scrutiny. Managers can no longer fall back on functional hierarchies or traditional ways of doing things to protect themselves. What they do and how they work is stripped bare for all to see.

This process creates a new sense of ambiguity. People are uncertain about their roles and unsure what they should be doing and with whom. This ambiguity covers a number of areas:

- Job definitions – changes in the scope and nature of job definitions are, for many, deeply unsettling and remove a prime reference point.
- Responsibilities – people are unsure what they are responsible for and to whom.
- Expectations – people are uncertain about what colleagues and the organisation expects from them.

DISAPPEARING LADDERS

An obvious adjunct to the process of ambiguity is the disappearance of career ladders. Organisations shorn of their vertical hierarchy can appear to offer little opportunity for progression. IBM UK chairman, Sir Anthony Cleaver, announced that his organisation was reducing its number of management tiers to a mere four. This, said Cleaver, 'means a maximum of one promotion every ten years and even this is for the one man who makes it to the top'.[7]

One life assurance company re-structured its customer servicing division. Team-based operations are now in place with three layers of management instead of the previous seven. Customer service representatives have replaced administrators and clerks, and they now have a different reward and performance appraisal system. But the opportunities for promotional advancement up the career ladder no longer exist. The new re-engineered way focuses on recognition through teamwork, with managers being elected by team colleagues. Adapting to the changes requires that the employees radically re-align their career expectations and measurements of success.

Those who plan to join the upwardly mobile and still believe in neat and well-ordered career structures are increasingly likely to be disappointed. The Institute of Management (IM) tracked the career development of over 800 UK managers from 1980 to 1992. IM found that sideway or downward moves among managers more than doubled during the period from seven per 100 managers in 1980–82 to nearly 15 per 100 in 1992.[8] 'As the pace of change accelerates, the idea of a progressive career within stable organisational structures is increasingly threatened,' says the IM report on the research. 'The structures which have traditionally supported rational long-term careers are being gradually replaced with more fluid organisations.' And it is people who are the most fluid of corporate resources.

The impression of instability is emphasised the IM's findings that managers are changing jobs more often. They are job hopping, often not on their own terms, in search of better jobs, but increasingly because of corporate re-structuring. Managers tended to change jobs in the 1980s for proactive reasons – personal and career development – but in the 1990s they are often reacting to change which has been imposed on them, whether by redundancy or relocation. Among the 800 managers included in the survey, 25 per cent of those who changed jobs in 1992 did so because of re-organisation – in the early 1980s the figure was eight per cent.

These dramatic changes in the way managerial careers develop pose questions which strike at the heart of the western managerial culture. 'Young managers were once shown career structures stretching ten or even 15 year ahead. Stay with us and this is where you can go, they were told. Companies simply can't say that now,' says Bill Hudson, one of the managers in the report.

For managers at the sharp end, the changing structure of careers is not easily understood. 'In the 1980s you could plan your career. There were a lot of opportunities. Now, you have to accept that the only way is not always up,' says a redundant manager who recently applied for a job working for someone he once managed.

Strangely, the insecurity has not yet transmitted itself to some managers. Trudy Coe, co-author of the survey, says: 'Managers have to be prepared and, at the moment, many appear complacent. They think their careers are safe.' Research carried out by IM in 1992 found that 40 per cent of managers anticipated that their next career move would be upwards. 'Managers need to look at their careers differently,' says Coe. 'They have to see sideways moves as an opportunity to develop the broad portfolio of skills they now need. In the past managers looked to organisations to shape their careers and skills for them, now the onus is on them. They need to be prepared for change and to recognise its potential benefits rather than regarding it as a threat.'

DISAPPEARING POWER BASES

The re-engineered organisation is, for many managers, nightmarish. Instead of being tangible it is elusively intangible. Functions are broken apart, some disappear from the organisation, sub-contracted to external suppliers. For the manager reared on the old functional certainties the process-based organisation is very difficult to manage. The vast majority of managers are not trained or equipped to manage in such an environment. Nor can they attend a short course to be converted from a functional to a process manager. Changing the way you work and think about your work is a process which is more likely to take months and possibly years than weeks and months.

It is not surprising that re-engineered companies often report that it is managers rather than grass roots employees who find the transition to process-based work most difficult. As part of its change to more flexible working, the car manufacturer Rover encountered resistance from white-collar workers reluctant to switch jobs to the assembly line. In November 1993, Rover called for 1,000 volunteers to make the change so that it could avoid compulsory redundancies among its 33,000 workforce. Only 60 clerical staff volunteered. The end-result is that the company is planning to recruit more workers to make up the short-fall.

Managers often feel threatened by the change, a reaction that is reasonable given the fact that many re-engineering initiatives involve management de-layering (BT, for example, has shed over 5,000 managers during its re-engineering programme, and a European oil manufacturing company estimates that it will lose 50 per cent of its middle managers during its re-engineering programme over the next few years). Unfortunately and inaccurately, re-engineering can be regarded as a euphemism for redundancy.

Research suggests that while companies have developed a wide range of supportive packages to help people who have been made redundant they – perhaps not surprisingly – often forget the worries and concerns of those who remain with the organisation. In a survey of 50 top UK companies in 1993, recruitment company Cedar International found that a massive 86 per cent had implemented redundancies in the previous year and, in addition, 36 per cent were operating rolling programmes spanning a number of years involving a significant proportion of the workforce. 'Acceptance of out-placement and counselling for people being made redundant is obviously to be welcomed, but this is only part of the equation,' says Cedar chairman Bill Pitcher. 'The psychological impact of redundancy programmes can be just as devastating on those remaining. If one looks at redundancy as a change mechanism, not a clear out, it is absolutely vital that the process of change is fully explored with, and explained to, those who remain. Unless companies capitalise on the changes they have made and motivate surviving employees to contribute positively to the business, real growth and increased profits are unlikely to be achieved.'

The second cause of uncertainty is the disruption and destruction of fiefdoms and power bases, which causes managers to fear loss of control and authority. Becoming process owners, rather than function heads, can also be difficult for managers. Rank Xerox UK has found that managers struggle to overcome their functional mentalities. Director of business management systems and quality, James Havard says: 'We are finding it very tough to get process ownership among our mangers. Intellectually, people can grasp very quickly the concept of the process organisation. Then they return to their job and say "Wait a minute, my job is in service; how can I work when I am not responsible for a third of what you are now asking me to do?" '[9]

Ambiguity and insecurity are often indistinguishable. Indeed, some organisations have identified insecurity as one of the most valuable aspects of process-based working. Western Provident Association, a private UK health insurance company, has re-engineered itself through building 'customer centric' IT systems around two core processes which enable employees to work in multi-skilled teams and handle any type of customer need. WPA chief executive Julian Stainton believes that creating a 'culture of insecurity' is what makes a process-based organisation keep constantly revitalising itself. 'If you are in an environment that is constantly changing, you have to keep pushing forward and moving the goal pasts,' he maintains.[10]

WPA people have their performance closely monitored on a daily basis and are clearly accountable for the process on which they work. Staff have to fill in detailed performance reports twice a day, detailing how long they have worked, the number of customer transactions, telephone queries dealt with, accuracy rates and the number of complaints received. WPA also uses object-oriented activity logs, which enables it to catalogue precisely every form of action or task, whether this is a telephone conversation, memo or letter. This means that people are entirely accountable for what they do; if any stage of a process breaks down, the company can pinpoint where and why this happened. Within two years WPA turned losses into profits; productivity rose by 100 per cent and, among many other statistics, the time to process a new policy was reduced from 45 to four minutes.

There is, however, a disturbing Big Brother element in such an approach. Insecurity is not a great motivator. In the short term it might yield some performance benefits, but pure fear is hardly a long-term solution. A more positive motivational approach is to link rewards and remuneration more closely to customer satisfaction or team performance. As we have seen the disappearance of career ladders can disturb set notions of how a person's career is likely to develop. The association between success and promotion and higher rewards needs to be replaced. At Cigna, for example, 15 per cent of individual salaries are related to team performance – this figure was decided by more junior staff. Cigna's first US re-engineering programme hit problems because it did not discuss rewards systems early enough.

MANAGING CONFLICT

Managers are unused to the rigorous and ceaseless questioning which re-engineering brings with it. Often they are extremely uncomfortable with the idea of their work being analysed in anything other than a superficial way. The potential for dissension and conflict is high. If, for example, a team is made up of an engineer, a customer development manager and a company accountant, some sort of conflict is inevitable – and often healthy. There are, and will be, basic misunderstandings. The manager might ask the engineer why he is doing something in a certain way. Reared on a diet of functional division, the engineer may well say that he has always done it that way and he knows more about engineering than the manager. To make teams work, however, mutual respect must exist or be developed. Managers have to learn to accept objective input from people they regard as outsiders. Richard Pascale estimates that 50 per cent of the time contentious issues are smoothed over and avoided, around 30 per cent lead to non-productive fighting and no resolution, while only 20 per cent are truly confronted and resolved.[11]

Harvard's Chris Argyris has examined in great depth the debilitating machinations of a firm of consultants. He found that the consultants, despite their learning and expertise, were adept at masking their errors and mis-judgements. Problems were routinely by-passed and covered up, one cover-up led to another and so on. Board meetings were spent discussing peripheral issues while major issues were routinely glossed over. Argyris' conclusion is that the more threatening a problem is to those responsible for solving it, the deeper it will be ingrained under layers of corporate camouflage. Argyris's cure is for organisations to start learning from the top down. Managers, no matter how senior they are, must candidly and clearly take responsibility for their errors of judgement as well as their triumphs.

WHAT NEW SKILLS DO MANAGERS NEED?

From being functional specialists, re-engineering thrusts managers forward to become sophisticated generalists, able to manage a pot-pourri of projects, people, resources and issues. For most managers to make the transition from doers to enablers involves the development of a number of central new skills:

- **Interpersonal skills** – managers change from supervisors to coaches. They are there to provide resources, answer questions and look out for the long-term career development of the individual. How they deal with people is key to their day-to-day success and to the progression of their career within the organisation.

- **Project management skills**[12] – as we have seen, implementing re-designed processes involves highly developed project management skills. Our experience suggests that today's project manager (more accurately referred to as a project leader) needs training in four key areas:
  - **Planning and controlling** – project leaders need to be able to use a variety of methods to ensure that they are keeping on schedule and within budget. Even more important, they need to be able to decide priorities for their objectives.
  - **Learning skills** – as most project leaders are working in an unfamiliar context it is crucial that they assimilate knowledge as rapidly as possible. This will enable them to adjust their plans and objectives and save valuable time and money. To do this, project leaders need to keep learning, planning, reviewing and changing.
  - **People skills** – project leaders need to be able to negotiate for vital resources; be able to influence people to gain their commitment, be able to listen to co-ordinate and control the project, and be able to manage stakeholders from throughout the business.
  - **Organisational skills** – project leaders need to be politically astute and aware of the potential impact of wider organisational issues. They should be adept at networking with senior employees, should understand how the organisation works, and should have a larger picture of the organisation's goals and necessary conditions.

- **Leadership and flexibility** – like any manager who works in a horizontal cross-functional and team-based environment, process owners need to coach employees and empower them to feel ownership of the process. This demands a flexible style of managing, with the manager sometimes giving firm directions in order to ensure that the process output conforms to customer expectations, while at other times stepping back and allowing team members to take decisions.

- **Managing processes** – those charged with making processes work require a great range of different skills. Process owners, to use the language of re-engineering, have to be able to manage the boundaries between different processes (which are deeply rooted in vagueness), understand who are the stakeholders in the process, and help establish and monitor appropriate process performance measurements. They also need to be able to operate confidently up, down and across the organisation's structure. This ability, to manage chameleon-like across the organisation, is especially important during the early stages of re-engineering when many of the functional vestiges of old processes remain in place.

- **Improving processes** – in the majority of process-based companies, managers are required to refine and improve their business processes on an on-going basis. They need to be able to use the tools of process simplification and re-design, which include benchmarking, process mapping tools (such as systems dynamics, flowcharting and activity diagrams) and require understanding of the potential business benefits of IT applications.

- **Managing strategy** – process ownership is not solely concerned with the nitty gritty of direct implementation. Managers need also to understand how their process aligns with strategic goals and performance measures. They have, for example, to have an understanding of the company's mission, competitive capabilities and core constituencies, as well as some of the basic principles of activity-based costing. This enables the process owner to understand fully and communicate the full benefits of re-engineering – the elimination of non-value-adding activities, the enhancement of value-adding activities, substantial gains in productivity and far greater market responsiveness.

- **Managing their own development** – to meet the new challenge requires managers to think beyond position and develop comprehensive general skills which will allow them to respond flexibly to organisational needs. It is not surprising, therefore, that people at all levels in organisations are seeing the opportunities for personal development. Indeed, it is increasingly regarded as a major part of what was once called the remuneration package.

THE DEVELOPMENT CHALLENGE

When it came to management development, managers were once pawns in the hands of the organisation. If the company thought a manager needed a particular skill they were speedily despatched on a suitable course. As their careers progressed, managers assembled an impressive list of courses they had attended – though what they actually learned was often infrequently measured. In some companies development is still regarded in these terms. The trouble is that the skills needed by managers in the 1990s are so broad-ranging that picking off skills is no longer enough. Managers and their organisations have to be more selective and focused when it comes to development.

As part of this growing trend, managers – and their companies – now realise that developing managerial skills and techniques is not simply the responsibility of the company. Managers, too, have a role to play in being proactive and identifying areas in which they need to develop. Today, instead of being pawns moved around by corporate might, managers are increasingly encouraged to examine their own strengths and weaknesses and to develop the skills necessary for the future. Rather than having their development mapped out for them, managers are managing it for themselves.

The growing awareness of the potential of self-managed development is, to some extent, prompted by companies committing themselves to ideas such as empowerment. There is also growing interest in the entire idea of management competencies – the skills which managers will require to manage successfully in the future. Even though many companies are now expressing an interest in self-managed development, the habits of a generation are hard to break. Managers fed on a diet of conscripted training are uneasy about having the burden of their own development thrust upon them. Being *sent* on a course is something you can complain about – sometimes with justification. It is completely different when you have to identify your own needs and the best methods of satisfying them.

There are other reasons why self-managed development is a difficult concept for many managers to come to terms with. Some point to a lack of motivation. Why, they say, should they develop themselves when their company offers little or nothing in the way of support or rewards? There is also a strong fear of failure. In some areas, training has traditionally been regarded as a last resort, an admission of inadequacy. Other managers are simply unsure of what to do. They don't know where or how to start the process and, even if they begin, don't know how to maintain momentum.

Another disincentive to following self-managed development is simple lack of knowledge. Managers may be unable – or perhaps unwilling – to identify areas in which they need to develop and have little or no knowledge of the myriad of techniques, approaches and activities at their disposal. When they are actually given the time, resources and support to look at their own development, managers quickly become excited, realising that there are opportunities rather than obstacles. For many it is an entirely new experience. Given two days on a training course to analyse their own development needs, it often takes more than a day for managers to come to terms with what they are doing. It can be a revelation.

At an individual level, managers are usually prompted to think about their own development through changes in their job. It could be that taking on a new project motivates them to examine closely the skills they require. A completely new job often encourages greater self-examination. Perhaps the most widespread stimulus in the current climate is the disappearance of layers of management from major organisations. As the upward rungs disappear, managers have to make sure they make the right moves sideways which bring them into contact with important and useful new skills.

The sceptical might suggest that self-managed development is an abdication of a company's responsibility, a means of shifting management development on to the already loaded shoulders of their managers. But if it is to work, self-managed development involves and relies on the participation of the manager's organisation. The company has a vital role to play, providing opportunities, support and resources. Fundamentally, however, it is the individual managers who have to take final responsibility and control. They can't do this in isolation. Companies can't abandon their managers to plough their own furrow. Also, people need and want to share and test ideas with others. Self-managed development revolves around relationships with a wide range of people – from colleagues on courses to mentors and coaches, from the manager's boss to family and friends. The key relationship, however, must be with the organisation.

Many managers already have and use such networks. The trouble is that they often don't realise that they exist or that they can use them. If you ask a manager whether he or she has a mentor, many will quickly reply that they don't. Further questioning often reveals that a senior colleague is and has been instrumental in shaping their career and skills development – they have simply overlooked this or don't recognise it as mentoring. In fact, self-managed development in many ways fully utilises relationships and resources which already exist. When managers set out to gather information about a particular topic they often don't know where to start. Yet, with guidance they can quickly uncover information and resources they have previously ignored or been unable to use.

It is also true that many managers have neatly compartmentalised their lives and refuse to acknowledge links between their home and working lives. Self-managed development can remove the barriers which prevent managers learning lessons in their private lives which might be useful in their business roles. It regards development as a continuous process taking all aspects of a person's behaviour and outlook rather than simply taking one small aspect of it.

Self-managed development offers a degree of flexibility which traditional management training fails to provide. There is no set timescale or approved way of doing things – self-managed development revolves around managers thinking about how they learn and what they need to know. Traditional courses are based on the idea of moving a manager to a stated destination – knowing more about a particular subject or acquiring a new skill. Once the destination is reached, the process is regarded as complete. Self-managed development emphasises the journey rather than the destination. After all, the skills and techniques you plan to acquire are constantly changing.

There are four fundamental elements of self-managed development. The first is *analysis*. Managers can use a variety of methods to help them to identify possible development issues. They might, for example, look at how performance reviews would help them and what form they could take. They might then move on to *reviewing* – thinking, in a structured way, about what the data is telling them about their learning needs. The third element is *planning* – how you intend to meet your development needs. This covers thinking through what course or other form of learning is most useful, where to go to do it and why it is necessary. Finally, there is *activity* – developing and taking part in the most appropriate vehicle for meeting the development need. There is nothing cut and dried about these stages. Managers can join the process where they think it is most appropriate for them. Flexibility, combined with responsibility, is the key.

Self-managed development is based on commonsense principles. Put simply, it is a matter of recognising what you can and can't do and then trying to improve your performance. Experience at many companies suggests that self-managed development is going to be an integral part of developing managers in the future, ensuring that companies retain their best people and acting as a replacement for traditional rewards packages.

TEAMWORKING

What is a team? Is a team simply a fancy word for a group of people? What is the difference between a team and a task force? What is the difference between a team and a committee? Is a team simply a group of people with different skills aiming for the same goal?

Despite the extensive literature about teams and teamworking, the basic dynamics of teamworking often remain clouded and uncertain. Teams only occur when a number of people have a common goal and recognise that their personal success is dependent on the success of others. They are all inter-dependent. In practice, this means that in most teams people will contribute individual skills, many of which will be different. It also means that the full tensions and counter-balance of human behaviour will need to be demonstrated in the team. It is not enough to have a rag-bag collection of individual skills. The various behaviours of the team members need to mesh together in order to achieve objectives. For people to work successfully in teams, you need people to behave in certain ways. You need some people to concentrate on the task at hand (**doers**). You need some people to provide specialist knowledge (**knowers**) and some to solve problems as they arise (**solvers**). You need some people to make sure that it is going as well as it can and that the whole team is contributing fully (**checkers**). And you need some people to make sure that the team is operating as a cohesive social unit (**carers**).

Teamworking: who's who?[13]

Solver

Role: helps the team to solve problems by coming up with ideas or finding resources from outside the team. Can see another way forward.
Characterised by: innovation, ideas generation, imagination, unorthodox, good networking skills, negotiates for resources.

Doer

Role: concentrates on the task, getting it started, keeping it going, getting it done or making sure it is finished. Some may focus on only one aspect of the task. Making sure it is finished is the most rare.
Characterised by: high energy, high motivation, push others into action,

assertiveness, practical, self-control, discipline, systematic approach, attention to detail, follow through.

Checker

Role: concern for the whole process, tries to ensure full participation while providing a balanced view of quality, time and realism.
Characterised by: prudence, reflection, critical thinking, shrewd judgements, causing others to work towards shared goals, use of individual talents.

Carer

Role: concern for the individuals in the team and how they are developing and getting along.
Characterised by: supportive, sociable, concerned about others, democratic, flexibility.

Knower

Role: provider of specialist knowledge or experience.
Characterised by: dedication, standards, focus.

For people to work well together you need both a range of specific skills or technical skills and a range of different human behaviours. When you look hard at people and how they behave when they are working in teams you find that in addition to the actual content of the work they are doing, they take on certain behaviours. Each person has a favourite way of behaving when they work with others. Modern management thinking suggests that you need a balance of behaviours for any change management activity, but you may wish to unbalance the team slightly in favour of the type of change you are trying to undertake.

It is also worth noting that for all the research which has been carried out into effective teamworking, teams remain a law unto themselves. Managers who sit down and play at human engineering by trying to select exactly the right sort of combination usually end up in a state of confusion. Often the teams that have worked in re-engineering programmes have come about spontaneously or include an unusual combination of specialists. The key to success does not appear to lie in the selection of team members – you only have to look briefly at team sports to find examples of talented individuals working poorly as a team. Instead, success is often characterised by the genuine granting of power and responsibility to teams so they can solve their own problems.

NEXT STEPS

1. WHAT DO SENIOR MANAGERS NEED TO DO?

Abandon the past . . . and the present

In discussing and carrying through any programme of change, a crucial dilemma soon surfaces. Who should be involved in the planning and implementation? Involving the most powerful senior managers at the planning stage invites them to protect their own patch. Ignoring them in the implementation phase risks their blocking plans they don't like. The existing structure guarantees their power through their control over the largest and best resources currently available.

The fact is that despite the protestations of annual reports, senior managers are often the strongest and most persuasive corporate force against the process of change. They are, after all, creatures of the organisation – some will have spent their entire careers working within a particular culture in a particular way. As a result, they are protective of their own sphere of influence, often unwilling to upset the corporate equilibrium and unlikely to become passionate advocates of any one idea. They are in favour of stability and more of the same – it has elevated them to the corporate heights.

In the 1990s, such conservatism or plain stagnation is a guarantee of failure. 'If the top is committed deeply to maintaining the *status quo*, there's no hope,' says P Ranganath Nayak, senior vice-president of consultants Arthur D Little.[14] Dr Ian Cunningham, director of the Centre for the Study of Change, says: 'The old planning models are no longer enough. You cannot plan for a revolution. Instead, companies and managers need to prepare; managers need to be quicker, more able and feel confident enough to buck trends and be different. While it is difficult for many managers to develop this ability, they have to remember that you make money by not going along with the market. When it comes to change management, managers no longer have the luxury of being able to learn from their mistakes. They have to get it right.'[15]

Compared to quality programmes, re-engineering requires a much heavier participation by senior management because it introduces emotional and political issues that can only be resolved at the highest levels. Senior management must take the lead with both types of programme. However, while quality programmes require commitment from the bottom of the organisation, re-engineering is always driven by leaders taking project management roles. This is certainly the case until new processes, work flows and potential benefits emerge and the processes stabilise. Managers obsessed with corporate strategy, which juggles assets, buys and sells businesses, think more about leveraged buyouts than about basic changes in the work they actually do, have little, if any, place in re-engineering. According to Dan Valentino, chief executive of Gemini Consulting, re-structuring involves the chief executive becoming 'a tyrant, sacrificing people on the altar of shareholder value'. But is has to be done. 'All working processes, and their associated systems, must be under constant review.'[16]

While re-engineering is a broad-ranging idea, senior managers have to ensure that its direction and momentum are maintained while, at the same time, sustaining commitment and implementation of nitty-gritty examination of processes. John Hagel of McKinsey calculates that the chief executive and several other senior managers must devote up to half of their time to re-engineering for its entire duration.

Becoming visionaries

'Most people think of the future as the ends and the present as the means, whereas, in fact, the present is the ends and the future the means,' observed organisational behaviourist Fritz Roethlisberger in an unfortunately neglected aphorism.[17] Re-framing involves changing the way people think about their businesses. Failure to achieve this is a common cause of senior executive failure. It is a major challenge to shake a company away from its past obsession. As we have seen, organisations are cautious, slow-moving creatures. Tyre companies, for example, are still likely to believe that success is reliant on how many tyres they produce and coal mines may assume that tonnage automatically equates with profitability. There is a growing catalogue of senior and well-respected managers who have lost their jobs as they have wrestled with re-framing the outlook of a large corporation. Recent years have seen John Akers at IBM, Bob Stempel at General Motors, Bob Horton at BP, and a number of others succumb. They failed, not because they are poor managers – their track records are impressive – but because implementing major change requires much more than the attention and commitment of a single executive. The entire organisation needs to be carried forward with them.

The problem encountered by Akers and the like was that though their vision of the future was ambitious, credible and possibly achievable, it did not seem so to their colleagues or subordinates. Instead, all that their colleagues could see was a long line of obstacles and impediments to achieving the distant goal. Re-engineering takes a different tack to this perennial problem. Instead of coming up with a destination (B) and then going back to the beginning (A) to consider how to get there, it establishes B and works backwards to re-create A.

THE OLD ROUTE FROM REALITY TO VISION:
Step One: create destination – B
Step Two: consider where you are now – A
Step Three: create a direct route from A to B

The flaws in this approach are increasingly evident. Constant change in markets and technology means that the destination is likely to be changing constantly. The traditional view begins with a static view – what do you know now, what are your skills – and sets about 'improving' them to reach the destination. Re-engineering's imaginary blank piece of paper begins with the future.

THE NEW ROUTE
Step One: create destination (continuously changing) – B
Step Two: work backwards identifying stages
Step Three: re-create where you are now – A

The logic is simple: by re-creating where you are now, you are already closer to your planned destination.

Creating a destination is the easy part – all the research and papers on the trouble companies have in making strategy happen are evidence of the prime difficulty in converting theory into practice. To work, re-engineering must address how such widespread change affects the policy of a business, its values and its beliefs. This requires the vision to be able to motivate people through a radical re-think of their roles and tasks and sustain them through its implementation. This also results in new roles and changes in organisation development, rewards resource allocation and management systems.

Managers must become visionaries creating and implementing strong and clear visions of the corporate future. In General Electric's 1990 annual report, chief executive Jack Welch mapped out the company's vision: 'Our dream for the 1990s is a boundaryless company . . . where we knock down the walls that separate us from each other on the inside and from our key constituents on the outside'. Banca di America e di Italia began its re-engineering programme by creating a vision of creating a paperless bank.

After initial enthusiasm for corporate visions in the 1980s, recent years have seen mounting scepticism about their real value. Often they appear overly ambitious, entirely unrelated to the current situation of the business. Senior managers must bridge the gap between the vision and the day-to-day reality.

WHAT DOES A VISIONARY DO?

- Must seem to have as much to lose by not leading you forward as you do.
- Must be able to give you hope when it seems impossible that you will find your way out.
- Must act out the vision and be a role model so that you can see it active and embodied and be able to copy or reproduce it.
- Must challenge and practise.
- Must appear to care personally.
- Must take from you offerings, ideas and efforts which lead towards the vision.

Communicating

'A threat that everyone perceives but no one talks about is far more debilitating to a company than a threat that has been clearly revealed,' Richard Pascale has observed. Research by the consulting firm, Ingersoll Engineers, cited the communication problems faced in change programmes. Communication both upwards and downwards is considered crucial.

'Frequently the downward is there, but the upward falls on deaf ears,' commented one manager in the survey of top UK directors. 'Attempts [to change] without communicating . . . lead to the suspicion of a hidden agenda,' said another. 'Communicating a clear plan superlatively well is central to creating the confidence for successful change,' says Brian Small, managing director of Ingersoll.[18]

Forums for communication need to be established at an early stage in any change programme, and maintained and enhanced as the process unfolds. N&P, for example, introduced fortnightly meetings, 'team events' at which all area staff receive updates from top management to gain their commitment to the entire process. If people have no role to play in the formulation of ideas and the design of new processes it is unlikely they will implement them consistently or convincingly.

THE QUESTIONS PEOPLE ASK

Managers clearly need to prepare themselves to provide satisfactory answers to wide-ranging and fundamental questions from people who work for them. Typically, these will include:

- Will my job description change?
- Will I lose my job?
- What is the project about?
- How long will it take?
- Who is in the project team?
- What exactly are you doing?
- Will it affect the way I do my job?
- Why are you doing it?
- Will it save the company money?
- What's in it for me?
- Who has asked for the project to be done?
- Why do we need all this documentation?
- Does this mean I am not doing my job correctly?
- Are you checking up on me?
- What do I have to do?
- How does the project fit in with the computer department?
- What is a business process?
- Does this mean I am going to end up with more work?

---

2. IDENTIFY STAKEHOLDERS

There is a sure way to fail in re-engineering: appoint managers who have little credibility to drive the process forward. This is surprisingly common. Companies may accept the potential merits of re-engineering, but are unwilling or unable to bring their best minds in to run the revolution. If managers lack credibility or simply lack the right communication or leadership skills, re-engineering will not get off the ground. EDS picked 150 people to begin a process of corporate change. They were selected for what the chairman and chief executive Les Alberthal called 'their ability to think outside the box'. In selecting them the emphasis was on having a spread of ages, people from throughout the world, different levels with different ways of thinking. They were then broken into five 'waves' of 30 to focus on different issues.[19]

The stakeholders in any change programme are many and varied. All have their own motivations and agenda – both hidden and open. Managing a re-engineering programme you can divide stakeholders into several categories:

People who you need as resources. These may, for example, include the IT department.

People whom you need to take along. Those in the company who need to be persuaded and talked round as their role is potentially vital.

People who are going to be affected by the change.

People on the sidelines who are watching the progress of the change. These may include institutional investors, shareholders and customers.

For a process leader it is particularly important to identify stakeholders from a personal perspective (see Table 14.1).

Most people will discover a number of things simply by completing the map in Table 14.1. First, there are more stakeholders and more important stakeholders than they initially thought there were. Second, there are a number of stakeholders who are absolutely critical to success. Third, there are a number of interested parties whom you may have thought of as stakeholders, but who can, in fact, be managed at a distance from the action.

It is worth ranking your stakeholders in terms of two groups. Those absolutely critical to both progress and success and those who are not. Usually, sponsors, end-users, core team members and key contacts fall into

Table 14.1

Stakeholders	In your team, or department	In your organisations	In external organisations
Who wants you to succeed?			
Who wants you to fail?			
Who is betting on you to succeed?			
Who is betting on you to fail?			
Who is supporting you visibly?			
Who is supporting you invisibly?			
Whose success do you affect?			
Whose success affects you?			
Who does your change benefit?			
Who does your change damage?			
Who can change happen without?			
Who can change not happen without?			

the first category. Then establish which stakeholders are mainly interested in the outcome of the change and those who are mainly interested in what happens during the project – some will fall into both categories.

Inside every stakeholder there is a human being who is making judgements about what you are doing. Some are concerned with the more tangible and fixed aspects of the change you are managing, while others are interested in the less tangible, more transient things with which you are concerned. The way they decide on whether you have succeeded is by measuring you against standards or criteria.

Soft criteria: these are often quite difficult to establish. People don't always divulge their soft criteria. They feel it is unprofessional to talk about the less tangible aspects of the work. Although people tend to talk about hard criteria – financial performance, for example – what they really value and remember is the soft criteria.

Away from work, people pay a lot of attention to soft criteria. Choosing a plumber, for example, people often rely on the judgements of friends and neighbours as to the trustworthiness and skill of the plumber.

There are a number of soft criteria which regularly feature in people's measure of success:

- *Empathy*. Stakeholders need to feel that managers see and feel the world from their point of view.
- *Reliability*. Stakeholders usually need to feel that you will do whatever you say you will.
- *Fault-freeness*. Small errors, even mistakes, can upset some stakeholders.
- *Honesty*. This is very valuable to stakeholders. They can feel comfortable about the process and don't feel they have to keep watching their backs.
- *Fun*. Most people like to combine work with enjoyment.
- *Aesthetics*. Many stakeholders like to be pleased with the appearance of things. Clear progress charts, for example, are popularly reassuring.
- *Political sensitivity*. Few, if any, stakeholders enjoy being dropped in it. Positions, status, responsibilities, empires and reporting lines need to be thought through.
- *Individual soft criteria*. With key stakeholders it is also necessary to establish their individual foibles and preferences. Individual soft criteria are governed by the value that the person holds dear. You need to establish their values.

General hard criteria: to establish the harder, more measurable, tangible criteria for success you need to answer the question: 'Why is this change being carried out?'

Financial contribution

- How much is the project to cost?
- Are we costing this as real money or internal transfers?
- How much revenue will the project generate?

- Does the project generate money itself or does it rely on further business activities?
- Are the sums of money substantial with respect to the whole organisation?
- What is the impact of over- or underspending?

Timeliness

- When does the change need to be complete by?
- What happens if it is late?
- What happens if it is early?
- Who is expecting to receive what we deliver and when?
- Is there a window of opportunity?
- Who or what is the window bounded by? Competitors? Legislation? Customers? Technology?

Business and technical objectives

- What objectives are definitely not in the scope of the project?
- What objectives are definitely within the scope of the project?

KEY POINTS

1. *Integrate hard and soft issues.* Processes cannot be regarded as people-free; they revolve around people understanding and implementing them consistently and efficiently.
2. *Transform culture.* Strike a balance between a healthy lack of complacency and acceptance of change, and insecurity at the ramifications of re-engineering.
3. Change attitudes so that people learn to thrive on the new turbulent environment rather than being intimidated by it.
4. Create an entirely new corporate culture which is built around change, flexibility and customers.
5. *Develop people.* Teach managers new skills so they have the necessary tools and techniques to make re-engineering happen. Encourage and enable managers to map out their own development needs and aspirations.

Notes

1 Skinner, C, 'Business process re-engineering', *Internal Communication Focus*, December 1993/January 1994.

2 KPMG, *Change Management*, KPMG, 1993.

3 'The technology pay-off', *Business Week*, 14 June 1993.

4 'Outsource boom for in-house services', *Financial Times*, 11 January 1994.

5 Michaels, A, 'Culture vultures', *Financial Times*, 19 July 1993.

6 Levi, J, 'Whessoe's culture change works wonders', *Management Today*, May 1993.

7 Dixon, M, 'The benefits of a switchable personality', *Financial Times*, 26 January 1994.

8 Institute of Management, *Are Career Ladders Disappearing?*, IM, Corby, 1993.

9 Devine, M, 'Radical re-engineering', *Directions*, September 1993.

10 Devine, M, 'Radical re-engineering', *Directions*, September 1993.

11 Pascale, R, 'The benefit of a clash of opinions', *Personnel Management*, October 1993.

12 Obeng, EDA, 'Avoiding the fast-track pitfalls', *Sunday Times*, 11 March 1990.

13 Obeng, EDA, *All Change!*, FT/Pitman, London, 1994.

14 Lorenz, C, 'Struggling with the curse of success', *Financial Times*, 22 October 1993.

15 Crainer, S, 'Better for the change', *The Times*, 30 September 1993.

16 Trapp, R, 'How to ride the winds of change', *Independent on Sunday*, 12 December 1993.

17 Roethlisberger, F, *Training for Human Relations*, Harvard University Press, Boston, 1954.

18 'Putting over the message', *Financial Times*, 3 September 1993.

19 Lorenz, C, 'Avoiding the IBM Trap', *Financial Times*, 15 October 1993.

5

BEYOND
RE-ENGINEERING

BEYOND THE QUICK-FIX

Management fads and fashions are notoriously fickle. It is likely that re-engineering will, after two or three years of popularity, slip out of the management agenda. Its advocacy of fundamental change makes this even more likely. At best, re-engineering is a means of improving effectiveness and productivity right across an organisation. There is already a disturbing tendency for organisations to hijack the idea of re-engineering and interpret it as a justification for mass redundancies. Numbers and costs are cut, and corporations proclaim themselves 're-engineered'. Re-engineering gurus are already bemoaning the fact that few organisations seem to have understood fully what the gurus are saying and that 're-engineered' organisations often mysteriously forget to re-engineer managerial processes. 'I can count on one hand the number of executives who have adopted a new style of empowerment,' James Champy has lamented.[1]

Re-engineering has also been bedevilled by an all or nothing approach. Writers and consultants have labelled re-engineering as a 'revolution' and propose a dramatic revolution where traditional and long-established practices are dramatically overturned. Perhaps they imagine the corporate equivalent of the French Revolution. In fact, re-engineering is as likely to be a quiet revolution – akin to pulling down the Berlin Wall.

The all-or-nothing approach distinguishes between business process re-engineering and business process re-design. While the former is the clean slate, revolutionary approach, the latter is regarded as an incremental adjustment more in keeping with the quality management concept of continuous evolutionary change. We believe this is a question of semantics, of little interest to managers and workers who have to cope with and manage change. The truth is that few, if any, corporations have the resources to commit themselves to full-scale re-engineering with its clean slate. 'Wide-scale re-engineering exacts extraordinary effort at all levels of an organisation. Without strong leadership from top management, the psychological and political disruptions that accompany such radical change can sabotage the project,' observed a group of McKinsey consultants in a *Harvard Business Review* article.[2]

Organisations which take the clean-slate route are usually those who are in a situation where a high-risk strategy is seen as the only escape. There are precious few examples of fully re-engineered multinationals (perhaps the best example is Asea Brown Boveri which, despite having 215,000 employees in 140 countries, has a mere three levels of management between the chief executive and the small teams dealing with the business). Instead, organisations are more likely to follow the path of process re-design which they can implement on a project-by-project basis. We believe that this approach is as revolutionary as full-blown re-engineering. It can enable organisations to take quantum leaps forward.

Another problem with re-engineering's surge in popularity is that, like many of its predecessors, it is being promoted as a corporate saviour, a one-stop quick fix. Re-engineering cannot be regarded as a catch-all solution to the problems of businesses in the 1990s. Implementation and interpretation varies from organisation to organisation. As we have pointed out, there can be no formula or recipe for success.

THE FACTS OF RE-ENGINEERED LIFE

All the theorising about re-engineering masks a number of simple messages which organisations have to take on-board if they are to cope with a future riddled with fear and uncertainty:

Your organisation needs to change. Managers may spend many hours discussing the need for change. They are wasting their time. All organisations need to change. Those that refuse to will perish. It is worth remembering that almost 40 per cent of the companies in the *Fortune 500* of ten years ago no longer exist. From the 1970 *Fortune* list 60 per cent have gone out of business or have been acquired. And, of the 12 companies which comprised the Dow Jones Industrial index in 1900, only General Electric still survives as a giant.

When Tom Peters and Robert Waterman wrote *In Search of Excellence* there were few complaints about their selection of 'excellent' companies. In

Peters' next book, he observed 'Excellence RIP' – the excellent companies had singularly failed to maintain their status. Such a fate is inevitable for those organisations which refuse to move forwards.

It doesn't matter who you are or how big you are. Corporate complacency is perhaps the biggest stumbling block to re-engineering. Companies tend to wait for change to affect them rather than being the instigators of change. Such apathy was at the heart of IBM's dramatic fall in fortunes.

Change while the going is good. The IT services company EDS has, on paper at least, little reason to instigate change. In 1992 it increased sales and net income by 16 per cent. By 1993 it was putting itself through a rigorous process of critical self-analysis. 'When you're successful the tendency is to start institutionalising it,' says EDS chairman and chief executive Les Alberthal. EDS has rejected the notions that:

- successful methods are self-perpetuating – all you have to do is more of the same;
- scale and resources enable large companies to weather changes in their market and industry.[3]

Time competitiveness is of the essence. For companies which have introduced true empowerment, teamworking, closer relationships with customers and engendered a sense of responsibility throughout the organisation, the end-result is most clearly characterised by enhanced time competitiveness. They are flexible and quick in all aspects of their business. Time-consuming tasks have been eliminated, as have delaying divides and pointless inspection. These are crucial additions to the competitive armoury of any organisation. In the new world order being quicker can no longer mean that you are more expensive – it is expected.

- Bell Atlantic used to take two weeks to a month to connect customers to the long-distance carrier of their choice. By the end of 1992 this was down to a few days and has been further reduced to a few hours.
- At AT&T a unit has cut its design-delivery cycle ten fold since 1991 – from 53 to five days.
- IBM Credit has cut from a week to four hours the amount of time it takes to approve and issue financing deals.

You need to change. On a personal level managers need to change. They have to develop new managerial skills if they are to play a full part in tomorrow's organisation. It is they who have to drive the changes forward.

IT CAN BE DONE

For the faint-hearted, there is some reassurance. Many companies from throughout the world have, and are, proving that radical alternatives to the traditional approaches of managers and organisations do actually work. They are not a costly indulgence.

Semco, a company in Sao Paulo, Brazil, provides a forceful rebuttal to those doubtful of the practicality and business-sense of true empowerment. Semco has been so successful in converting empowerment to best practice that every week groups of executives from leading multinationals visit its factory in a non-descript industrial complex. The architect behind Semco's revolution is Ricardo Semler. When he took the company over from his father he spent the first day firing 60 per cent of the top management. 'We've taken a company that was moribund and made it thrive, chiefly by refusing to squander our greatest resource, our people, says Semler. Semco has managed to buck Brazil's commercial chaos, hyper-inflation, and recession, to increase productivity seven-fold and profits five-fold.

Semler has eliminated meaningless layers of management. Jobs have become merged. Visitors, for example, immediately notice that there is no receptionist – everyone at Semco is expected to meet their own visitors. There are no secretaries or personal assistants. Managers do their own photocopying, send their own faxes and make their own coffee. Semco takes empowerment to previously unimagined frontiers. 'A few years ago when we wanted to relocate a factory, we closed for a day and everyone piled into buses to inspect three sites,' says Semler. 'Their choice hardly thrilled the management, since it was next to a company that was frequently on strike. But we moved in anyway.'

Everyone at Semco has access to the company's books; managers set their own salaries; shopfloor workers set their own productivity targets and schedules; workers make decisions once the preserve of managers; even the distribution of the profit-sharing scheme is determined by employees.

'There are some companies which are prepared to change the way they work. They realise that nothing can be based on what used to be, that there is a better way. But 99 per cent of companies are not ready, they are caught in an industrial Jurassic Park,' says Ricardo Semler. 'The era of using people as production tools is coming to an end. Participation is infinitely more complex to practise than conventional unilateralism, but it is something which companies can no longer ignore.'

Semler admits that empowerment demands that mangers become adept at biting their tongues when decisions don't go their way. 'There are a lot of people at Semco whose styles I don't actually like. I wouldn't have recruited them but quite clearly they do their jobs effectively – otherwise people wouldn't support them.' As part of Semco's revolution, Ricardo Semler has, to a large extent, become redundant. The chief executive's job rotates between five people. Diminished power is clearly not something which fills him with sadness – instead, it is confirmation that the Semco approach works. 'I haven't hired or fired anyone for eight years or signed a company cheque. From an operational side I am no longer necessary, though I still draw a salary because there are many other ways of contributing to the company's success,' he says.

Indeed, Semler believes that what many consider the core activity of management – decision making – should not be its function at all. 'It's only when bosses give up decision making and let their employees govern themselves that the possibility exists for a business jointly managed by workers and executives. That is true participative management. Really, the work is only 30 per cent completed. In the long term, success will come when the system forgets me and becomes self-perpetuating.'[4]

SUCCESS FACTORS

Semler's key message is that what he has done cannot be copied or emulated. The solutions found by a Brazilian manufacturer do not automatically translate to other organisations in other environments. But, from the growing wealth of material on organisations which have made such radical changes work, a few general characteristics can be established for organisations likely to succeed. They are characterised by the following:

Geared to change. These organisations have undergone the central realisation that they need to change. They are not half-hearted in this – they don't add on a crucial 'but' or seek to avoid the necessity. They are frank and open about this fundamental need.

Obsession. There is no half-way house if an organisation is genuinely committed to change. The senior managers, who drive the process forward, must become obsessed with achieving radical change so that they can convince others in the organisation of its necessity. The message must continually be pushed home. One managing director we talked to was especially proud of how he had destroyed functional silos in his organisation. To prove the point he walked down the corridor and asked in every office, 'What do we do with functional silos?' The responses were consistent and would not have amused pacifists. This sort of evangelical selling of the idea is all-important.

Opening minds. Companies which have succeeded in re-engineering have managed to shake off narrow functional and organisational views of the world. They do not make assumptions about what customers need or what employees think about a new strategy, but actively and continuously canvass ideas and opinions from inside and outside the organisation. They recognise that lessons, ideas and insights can be garnered from a huge range of people and organisations. The outside world is seen in a positive light, as a source of inspiration, rather than an irritation. The company does not know best, but seeks to know more. They aggressively search out new avenues where improved performance can be achieved.

Recognise and value core constituencies. These organisations understand and continually try to understand more about the core constituencies of their business.

Regard re-engineering as a positive opportunity. Change and re-engineering are regarded in a highly positive way. Instead of feeling imperilled and impelled to change, the organisation regards change as an opportunity. Those that see change as a necessity forced upon them by external forces are unlikely to have the commitment necessary to make genuine change happen.

Even this list of some of the characteristics apparent in organisations which have had some measure of success is daunting. It is by no means exhaustive. The challenge to an organisation should never be under-estimated, but whether organisations capitalise on re-engineering or not, they are left with an uncertain future in which they have to find their own solutions to perpetual process of change. Failure to come to terms with change will lead to corporate failure – of that there can be little doubt.

Notes

1 Champy, J, 'Time to re-engineer the manager', *Financial Times*, 14 January 1994.
2 Hall, G, Rosenthal, J & Wade, J, 'How to make re-engineering really work', *Harvard Business Review*, November–December 1993.
3 Lorenz, C, 'Avoiding the IBM trap', *Financial Times*, 15 October 1993.
4 Semler, R, *Maverick!*, Century, London, 1993.

GLOSSARY

The language of re-engineering

'A' Configuration   When laid out on a **space time map** the flows from inputs to outputs forms an 'A' shape as we move from a wide range of **inputs** to a limited range
of **offerings.**

Aura   A term describing the non-tangible attributes of the offering for which **customers** or **clients** will willingly pay money. This covers the strength of the brand attributes, the 'feel good' factor associated with the purchase, the 'air of quality, reliability', etc. For example, it's the difference in price between buying a branded product and a non-branded equivalent.

Client   An individual or organisation which wants to use the **output** of the **process** – the **offering** – or the individual or organisation which wants to use the **output** of the **project** – the **deliverables**. Clients tends to describe an individual or organisation with a mutually agreed role that they drive at least the output of the process and sometimes the process itself.

Closed Process   A process in which what the process is to provide and how it is to work are established.

Constituency   A constituency is a group of **stakeholders** who play the same role with respect to the **process** or **project.** So governmental bodies, regulators and legislators play the same role in establishing and monitoring the **necessary conditions** that the organisation must meet.

Constraint   A constraint is *anything* that limits the performance of a process with respect to its goals. It may be physical, such as a resource shortage, computer processing speed, a slow machine or a lack of people with a requisite skill, or it may be mental or non-physical such as a rule, policy, assumption, poor quality of information or even a lack of will.

Consumer   An individual or organisation after which the **process** comes to an end. They do not pass on the **offering** in any shape or form. The **client** or **customer** may often be the consumer.

Customer (*also see* Internal customer)   An individual or organisation which exchanges money for the **offering** provided by the organisation. The customer *may* be invited by the organisation to drive the **output** of the **process** or the process itself.

End consumer (*see* Consumer)

Internal customer   In internal organisation transactions it is normal for one party to do the work while the other party receives the **output** of that stage of the **process.** The party receiving the work is known as the internal customer. In this case no money changes hands although in some cases there may be internal transfer charges of 'funny money'.

Internal supplier (*also see* Internal customer)   In internal organisation transactions it is normal for one party to do the work while the other party receives the **output** of that stage of the **process.** The party doing the work is called the internal supplier.

Necessary conditions   The minimum standards, conditions or capabilities which an organisation must meet in order to be allowed to pursue its goals.

Offering   The combination of goods, services and **aura** produced by the process, made available to the **constituents.**

Open Process   A process for which either what is to be achieved or how it is to be done is not completely clear.

Output (*also see* Offering)   The materials, information or change to people caused by the **process.**

Points of constraint (*also see* Constraint)   Anything which has a very significant impact on reducing an organisation's ability to meet its goals. A point of constraint can be a material processor (e.g. a machine), information or an information processor (e.g. a policy or computer), or a person.

Process   A process is a group of activities that cause change to happen primarily along the space axis of the space time map. Change occurs through *simultaneous* activities.

Process design   This covers both the high-level selection of the standard process operations to be applied and the selection of appropriate business process configurations (**V**, **A** or **T** on the **space time map**).

Process owner   The person given project responsibility for the management and implementation of a particular process re-design.

Process re-engineering   Process re-engineering describes the method by which physical or mental **recipe**-induced **constraints** are eliminated from the organisation and re-established in a way which better meets the goals of the organisation.

Process tidying   Process tidying is a method by which existing flows of people, information and materials are mapped and streamlined by identifying opportunities for eliminating dead ends, *ad hoc* activities and duplication.

Process tinkering   Process tinkering is a method by which organisations find short-cuts in their processes or identify more user-friendly ways of doing work. In general, process tinkering does not change the overall process, nor does it seek to move **points of constraint.**

Process vision The translation of organisational goals into measurable process terms.

Project A project is a special limiting case of process in which change happens primarily along the time axis of the **space time map.** Change occurs through *sequential* activities. It encompasses the definition of project objectives by recon-ciling the objectives of a diverse group of **stakeholders**, then planning, co-ordinating and implementing the activities necessary to achieve those objectives to the satisfac-tion of the **stakeholder group**.

Recipe An organisation develops a recipe when its past strategy becomes fused with the current organisational culture. People begin to believe that they know how things are done and stop questioning the assumptions behind their thoughts and actions.

Space time map Change described in terms of two axes of space and time. A space time map may show the locations and tasks carried out by people, machines or information processing equipment.

Sub-processes Specific processes underlying the four top-level **processes**, e.g. investment process, marketing process, etc.

'T' Configuration When laid out on a **space time map** the flows from **inputs** to **outputs** forms a 'T' shape as we move from a wide range of inputs to a limited range of intermediates or modules and then on to a wide range of **offerings.**

Unit operations High level process stages: transformation; identification; unification; consistency; movement; holding; and offering.

'V' Configuration When laid out on a **space time map** the flows from **inputs** to **outputs** forms a 'V' shape as we move from a limited range of inputs to a wide range of **offerings.**

FURTHER READING

Davenport, T, *Process Innovation: Re-engineering Work Through IT*, HBS Press/ McGraw Hill, New York, 1993.

Goldratt, EM, *The Goal: A Process of Ongoing Improvement*, Gower, Aldershot, 1984.

Hammer, M & Champy, J, *Re-engineering the Corporation: A Manifesto for Business Revolution*, Nicholas Brealey, London, 1993.

Hanan, M, *Tomorrow's Competition*, AMACOM, New York, 1991.

Harrington, HJ, *Business Process Improvement*, McGraw Hill, Maidenhead, 1991.

Hodgson, P & Crainer, S, *What Do High Performance Managers Really Do?*, FT/Pitman, London, 1993.

Johansson, HJ, *et al.*, *Business Process Re-engineering*, John Wiley, Chichester, 1993.

Keen, PGW, *Shaping the Future: Business Design Through Information Technology*, Harvard Business School Press, Boston, 1991.

Obeng, EDA, *All Change!*, FT/Pitman, London, 1994.

Sadler, P, *Managing Talent*, FT/Pitman, London, 1993.

Ward J, Griffiths P & Whitmore P, *Strategic Planning for Infomation Systems*, John Wiley, Chichester, 1990.

Womack, JP, Jones, DT & Roos, D, *The Machine That Changed the World*, Macmillan, Basingstoke, 1990.

Zuboff, S, *In the Age of the Smart Machine: The Future of Work and Power*, Heinemann, Oxford, 1988.

INDEX

INDEX